The Dal Pozzo Copies of the Palestrina Mosaic

Helen Whitehouse

BAR Supplementary Series 12
1976

British Archaeological Reports

122, Banbury Road, Oxford OX2 7BP, England

B.A.R. Supplementary Series 12, 1976: "The Dal Pozzo Copies of the Palestrina Mosaic"

ISBN 9780904531480 paperback
ISBN 9781407327242 e-book
DOI https://doi.org/10.30861/9780904531480
A catalogue record for this book is available from the British Library

This book is available at www.barpublishing.com

CONTENTS

LIST OF FIGURES

***Please note that the foldout is now available to download from www.barpublishing.com/additional-downloads.html**
The original foldout has been reduced in size to match the A4 format of this book, the image is therefore not as clear as the original foldout. Please refer to the original foldout via the download for the original content.

ACKNOWLEDGEMENTS

The drawings from the Royal Library, Windsor Castle, are reproduced by gracious permission of Her Majesty the Queen.

I am most grateful to Professor Martin Robertson for discussing this work in progress and for reading the draft version of the text; Mrs. Sheila Somers Rinehart and Sir Anthony Blunt for assisting me with enquiries about the authorship of the copies; and especially my former teacher Professor John R. Harris for his help and encouragement with this, as with many other things.

Photographs: Fig. 19b: by courtesy of the Staatliche Museen zu Berlin; Figs. 1b & c, 2b, 3b, 4b, 6b, 7b, 9b, 10b, 15b and 19c: Alinari; fold-out plate: Scala.

I

THE BACKGROUND TO THE COPIES

Second only perhaps to the Alexander mosaic from Pompeii in the amount that has been written about it, the large Nilotic landscape known as the Palestrina or Barberini mosaic has been the object of studies by scholars from Athanasius Kircher on, a favourite illustration in books on ancient art, beginning with the seventeenth-century compendia, and even, in more recent times, the subject of a documentary film. For "this very instructive piece of antiquity", as Thomas Shaw dubbed it,[1] not only was one of the first Roman mosaics to come to light, and that at a time when serious antiquarian study was just beginning, but is also remarkable for its size and quality, and the novelty and interest of its subject matter. Moreover, its proximity to one of the famous temples of antiquity and its apparent connection with a crucial passage in Pliny's Natural History have assured it of a prominent place in Roman art history.[2]

Detailed study of the mosaic has always been hampered by the fact that we have no exact idea of its original form, only the certain knowledge that it has been much restored since the time of its discovery and probably contains inaccuracies. Scholars writing about it have often lamented the apparent loss of the eighteen drawings known from seventeenth-century sources to be in the Museum Chartaceum of Commendatore Cassiano dal Pozzo and to show the mosaic in its pre-restoration state, and even perhaps in its original integral form. The copies are in fact still in existence, for in the mid-eighteenth century they passed, together with the bulk of Dal Pozzo's great collection of antiquarian drawings, from Italy to England, and were incorporated in the collections of the Royal Library, Windsor Castle. Apart from their merits as drawings after the antique, they are of the highest interest for the light they shed on the Palestrina mosaic; while resolving some of the old questions, such as whether Dal Pozzo's artist was drawing the whole mosaic or pieces of it, and hence whether any copy was made of it in its entirety, they pose some new ones, notably regarding the incorrect arrangement of the restored mosaic. These are the problems with which the present monograph is primarily concerned, and except in so far as they are vital to some point concerning the relation of the drawings to the mosaic neither the many questions raised by its subject matter nor the important problem of its dating will be considered in detail here. It may however be appropriate to begin with a description of the mosaic and a brief survey of the current state of opinions regarding it, and to follow this with an account of its finding and subsequent fortunes, for the drawings' particular value stems from the fact that the mosaic has undergone several restorations, and the earlier part of its history since discovery is not altogether easy to trace.

The Palestrina mosaic originally formed the pavement of an apsidal recess at the north end of a large rectangular building situated behind the area occupied

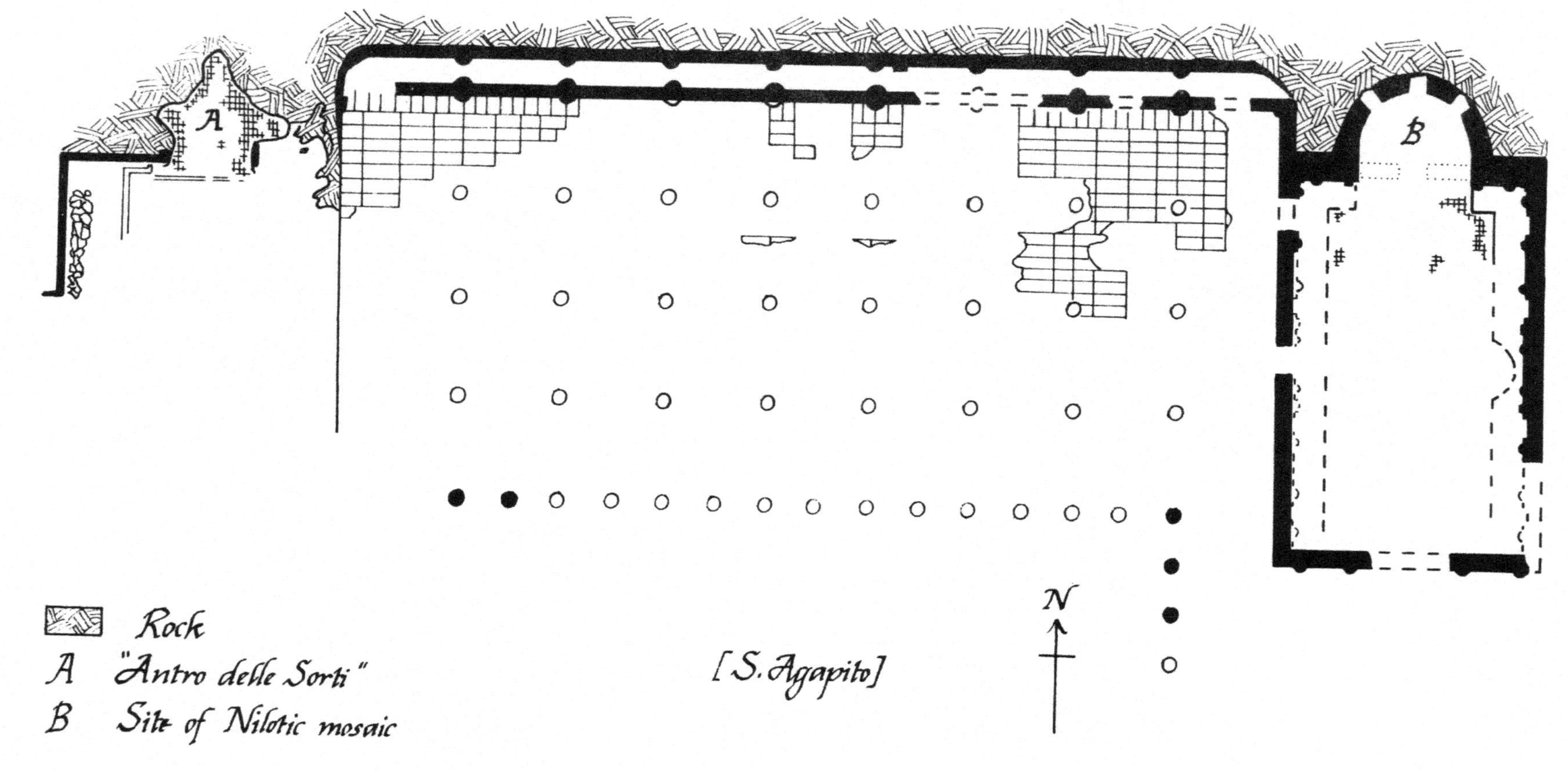

A. The lower complex at Palestrina, after Delbrueck and Bradshaw.
Scale 1:400

by the forum of Praeneste (Palestrina) and below the seventh level of the Temple of Fortuna Primigenia.[3] Much of this structure remains visible today, incorporated in the fabric of the building, now the Seminary of S. Agapito, which grew up on the site. South-west of the Seminary is the Cathedral of S. Agapito, and the surrounding area is extensively built over with private houses; behind the Cathedral and west of the Seminary is an open court, formerly colonnaded and covered, and in the north-west corner of this a grotto, the so-called Antro delle Sorti, hollowed out of the rock, which was covered with mortar in imitation of stalactites, and paved with another mosaic, the Fish Mosaic discovered in 1863.[4] The nature of the basilica-like construction which contained the Nilotic mosaic has never been satisfactorily defined, and the question of whether this whole lower area with its two mosaics is part of the temple above, or completely separate from it and secular, remains unresolved.[5] The building consists of a rectangular hall entered on the long western side (see plan, Fig. A); around it ran a podium, and above this the surface of the wall was broken up by a series of niches alternating with engaged columns. Light would have come from windows set higher up, and the floor was paved with plain white mosaic bordered at the outer edges with black. The vaulted apse which the Nilotic mosaic occupied is 4.35 m deep and 6.87 m wide at the opening, with three niches let into the circumference at floor level, and two smaller ones higher up.[6] Like the "Antro delle Sorti", the apse was cut into the rock of the hill-side behind and similarly treated with artificial grotto-work; the roof would continually have dripped water onto the surface of the mosaic below, which was set at a slightly lower level than the floor of the main part of the building.[7]

The mosaic is a large-scale work depicting, in bird's-eye view, a landscape consisting of two distinct halves: an upper rocky terrain inhabited by exotic animals, the majority of which are identified by their names in Greek, and a lower marshy prospect dotted with temple complexes of Egyptian and Graeco-Egyptian form and humbler buildings such as tower-houses, huts, reed shelters and a dovecote. Between the tracts of land the water is alive with boats large and small, from one-man papyrus skiffs to cargo boats, a warship and an elaborate cabined hunting vessel. The mosaic is peopled in the upper part with dark-skinned hunters, in the lower with peasants in working dress, priests in distinctive Egyptian garb, civilians and soldiers, the latter group taking part in a scene which is given some prominence in the foreground. The picture before us is Egypt and the Nile, and we are being treated to a graphic "map" of the country from the highlands of Ethiopia where the river rises to the marshes of the Delta where it debouches into the sea. From the expanse of water, the quantity of shipping, the festival decorations on the buildings and the scenes of ceremonies and carousing we can deduce that the country is being portrayed at the season of inundation, the time when its "great wonders" are to be beheld — "the same man both sailor and husbandman on one tract of land, and cattle grazing with cargo boats but a little way off, and in an instant an island where before there was a city on dry land".[8]

Although the mosaic falls into that category of Roman landscape depiction known as Nilotic, it is to date unique in much of its subject matter and stands apart from the mass of these often rather lighthearted Egyptianising scenes. At the same time it contains more specifically Egyptian material than any of the examples of "sacro-idyllic" landscape to which it is also to some extent related.[9] Wider in scope than either class to which it might be assigned, it has the air of an important work, and the diversity of its contents prohibits a neat categorization of it as a topographical, cartographical, zoological, genre or religious work, though all these different elements are present in the composition. To many eyes it has a distinctly Hellenistic look; it is sometimes urged as proof of an Alexandrian origin for Nilotic landscapes, and has often been a key work in attempts to trace the evolution of landscape representation in general in Roman art.[10] It would be most satisfactory if it could be dated accurately, but after three hundred years of discussion the final word on this vital point has yet to be said.

The mosaic was removed from its original site in an age of unscientific excavation, and there is no clear archaeological evidence by which it might be dated, in conjunction with the building in which it was found, to the first quarter of the first century B.C. In the absence of any such proof secondary arguments have been adduced from the style and content of the composition and from certain extraneous factors. The dates thus achieved range from the time of Sulla, c. 80 B.C., to the early third century A.D., with the bulk of opinions settling in favour of either a Sullan or a Hadrianic dating, and the greater number favouring the Sullan.[11] The mosaic could thus be seen as contemporaneous with its immediate surroundings, including the "Antro delle Sorti" mosaic, and an integral part of the dictator's architectural re-embellishment of the area after his defeat of the supporters of Marius in Palestrina in 82 B.C. Since the seventeenth century a link between Sulla and the mosaic has been inferred from a statement in Pliny's account of the development of mosaic floors in Italy:

> "Lithostrota coeptavere iam sub Sulla; parvolis certe crustis exstat hodieque quod in Fortunae delubro Praeneste fecit." (Mosaic pavements began as far back as the time of Sulla; in fact, one made of tiny scraps of stone, which he had laid in the sanctuary of Fortuna at Praeneste, exists to this very day.)[12]

If this passage refers to the Nilotic mosaic then we must assume that Pliny is using the words "lithostroton" and "parvolis crustis" in the sense of "opus tessellatum" and "tesseris". This interpretation of his terminology is by no means universally accepted, and it seems better to leave this vexed passage out of the dating question.[13] Stylistic parallels have been drawn between the mosaic and other works datable to the early to mid-first century B.C. — the fragmentary Nilotic landscape frieze from the Villa dei Misteri at Pompeii,[14] the mosaics from the Casa del Fauno at Pompeii, among which the tripartite Nilotic scene shows particularly close similarities,[15] and the Odyssey frieze from the Esquiline, Rome, dated c. 50-40 B.C. and seen by some as a form of landscape depiction related to that of the Palestrina composition but subsequent to it.[16]

Against this early dating it has sometimes been argued that a work so blatantly concerned with Egypt could have found no place in Italy before the Roman conquest of that country in 30 B.C. But other Roman Nilotic material datable pre-30 B.C. demonstrates that tastes in interior decoration were influenced by it well before then.[17] Some of the later datings proposed have been motivated by the desire to place the mosaic within a Roman historical context and link it to some specific visit of a distinguished person or an emperor to Egypt — thus the mid-first century B.C. (Pompey or Julius Caesar)[18] or post-30 B.C. (Augustus);[19] and most especially, the time of Hadrian, the latter's reign marking both the apogee of the fashion for things Egyptian in Roman art and also a revival in the art of polychrome mosaic.[20] But the various efforts to identify figures in the mosaic with famous Romans have been no more convincing than the wilder attempts to see Helen and Menelaus or Alexander the Great pictured therein;[21] and it is likewise hard to accept the proposed identifications of some of the rather generalised "type" buildings with specific Egyptian sites.[22] The latest dating, to the early third century A.D., was derived from an apparent link between the contents of the mosaic and the zoological writings of Aelian, who served as a priest at Palestrina in the time of Septimius Severus; but it is a moot point whether Aelian might have influenced the mosaic, or the mosaic Aelian, and points of congruence between his text and the animals in the mosaic could be explained by use of the same source material in either case.[23]

Stylistically this ultimate dating is hard to accept, and it might be prudent to conclude with Marion Blake that the mosaic "may have been laid at any time between Sulla and Hadrian".[24] When it is compared with the whole range of Nilotic landscapes, however, it finds its closest correspondence among those examples which seem to belong to the early stages of that genre in Roman art.[25] In addition it displays in pristine form many details of flora, fauna and architecture which appear elsewhere transmuted by the craftsman's non-comprehension into debased and sometimes nonsensical versions of the original;[26] it must therefore be either an early work in this style or a later one derived from a source far superior to those of its contemporaries. The fact that certain details can be paralleled in Ptolemaic or in the latest native Egyptian art but not in other examples of Roman Egyptianising art favours the early date.[27] Viewed within the contexts both of Nilotic scenes and of landscapes in general, the Palestrina mosaic would seem to occupy a place in the first century B.C., and the Sullan dating may perhaps be the most tenable.

The mosaic seems to have been chanced upon for the first time between the years 1588 to 1607, when the area in which it lay served as the cellar of the building which had taken shape on the remains of the apsidal hall, then the Bishop's Palace belonging to the adjacent Cathedral of S. Agapito.[28] But the earliest serious antiquarian interest in it dates from 1614, when Prince Federico Cesi, one of the four founders members of the Accademia dei Lincei, came to Palestrina, at that time the property of the Colonna family, to celebrate his marriage to his first wife, Artemisia Colonna. His enthusiasm was aroused alike by the considerable remains of the temple, whose terraced structure was still visible, and by the mosaic, and he ordered architects to draw and reconstruct the former, and also had drawings made of the latter. Cesi doubtless spread word of these "finds" to his fellow Lincei and other antiquaries, and he seems to have been the first to make the connection between the mosaic and the passage in Pliny's Natural History (quoted above, p. 4) which has entered into, and perhaps obscured, all discussions of the mosaic's possible date ever since.

The passage appears at the beginning of an account of the temple and the mosaic seemingly written by Cesi himself. The account was subsequently incorporated, with several omissions and interpolations, in a history of Praeneste written by Giuseppe Maria Suares, who, until becoming Bishop of Vaison in 1633, was librarian to Cardinal Francesco Barberini. The writing of the Praenestes Antiquae Libri Duo occupied Suares intermittently for two decades, the first book appearing in 1640 and the second (which contains this passage), plus addendum or "mantissa", as Suares styled it, in 1655. Suares is also the source of the most detailed contemporary information we have about the drawings of the mosaic in Cassiano dal Pozzo's possession, and his account of them has provided the foundation for subsequent work on the apparently missing copies. The alterations which he made to Cesi's description were examined in detail by Dante Sante Pieralisi, the Barberini family's librarian, who published a monograph on the mosaic in 1858.[29] Pieralisi found the original of the description in the family's archives: the manuscript was not in Cesi's hand, but a heading written by Suares himself stated that it was a copy of a letter of Cesi's made by his fellow Lynceus Francesco Stelluti, and given to Suares by Stelluti in 1637.[30] In the account Cesi mentions having seen the mosaic at the time of his marriage, and comments on the difficulty of viewing it properly in its dark and dank situation:

> "... But you may have an example of an extant lithostroton, the prototype of which you have had by reason of the Praenestine Fortune herself. Many indeed are the things to be seen in it, composed apparently of little chips of stone and cut fragments with assiduous attention to detail and painstaking care. At the site itself it was possible to see or draw only by torchlight and with water poured over [the surface of the mosaic] to aid visibility, and the washing down repeated frequently. There are various representations of men and beasts; Elephant, Rhinoceros, the names written out in some special letters; and in the water there are ships — you may behold these things meticulously portrayed, one by one, at the home of our fellow Lynceus Cavaliere Cassiano dal Pozzo, noted alike for his erudition and excellence,"[31]

In addition to incorporating this account in his book, Suares included a brief inventory of the Dal Pozzo copies of the mosaic in the mantissa, and, as will be seen later, this list is of crucial importance.

We next hear of the mosaic during the years 1624-6, when the then Archbishop of Palestrina, Andrea Peretti, began the process of having it removed piecemeal from the basement of the Bishop's Palace and sent to Rome "without either a plan or a drawing being made of it".[32] The move was not popular with the townsfolk,[33] and his successor Domenico Ginnasi halted the transfer of the fragments while some probably still remained in situ. In 1630, the feud of Palestrina was sold by the Colonna to the Barberini. In the meantime, the pieces of the mosaic in Rome passed from Peretti's heir, Francesco Peretti, to Cardinal Lorenzo Magalotti, who in turn gave them to his nephew, Cardinal Francesco Barberini. Magalotti kept one piece, which was subsequently replaced in the mosaic by a copy.[34]

Most of this information is recorded in a manuscript contained in a miscellany of Cassiano dal Pozzo's papers in Naples. The note on the mosaic dates from 1642, and after describing the Magalotti-Barberini transfer and Magalotti's retention of one piece, it goes on to say:

> "... the which piece Cardinal Barberini had re-made, following an exact copy in oils which Vincenzo was commissioned to make and which was in the household, by Giovan Battista Calandra of Vercelli, an expert mosaicist who restored the other pieces of the said mosaic and having brought them back to Palestrina by order of the said Signor and joined them together as best he could with the assistance of drawings belonging to the household, he put it into service again in the paved floor of a room in the said place in Palestrina. Calandra found it expedient to make use of various breccias found in the neighbourhood of Palestrina both for re-making the said missing piece and for restoring the others." [35]

The mosaic was sent back to Palestrina in 1640,[36] and a crucial fact about its return journey not contained in the above account is found in a rough draft of a letter among papers concerning Suares' history in the Barberini archives. The letter, which congratulates Suares on the publication of Praenestes Antiquae Libri Duo and so must belong to c. 1655, gives a description of the mosaic's passage from Peretti to Barberini; the latter –

> "... having ordered that [the mosaic] should be packed in boxes and replaced in the Palazzo at Palestrina, the boxes had been propped the wrong way round with the result that they had crushed and dislodged the whole mosaic; but with the drawings already executed by the inestimable Cav. Cassiano dal Pozzo and the lengthy care and great skill of .... Calandra it was all put together again; and Taddeo Barberino having appropriated the hemicycle[37] ... for the construction of a room, there being a large niche, platform or apse, what you will, left over in that, he put the said lithostroton back there, so well restored that not even the tiniest stone is missing from it, nor might there be one dislodged or put out of the original order...." [38]

Thus we know that the mosaic suffered considerable damage, and underwent extensive restoration before being placed in the Palazzo Barberini in the early 1640s.[39] A few pieces remaining in situ which had not been taken to Rome by Peretti were apparently replaced in the mosaic at this point. One of Suares' interpolations in the Cesi/Stelluti account records the fact that Cardinal Francesco Barberini had the fragments of the mosaic collected and drawn,[40] and an unpublished letter of Suares' cited by Pieralisi records gratitude to the Cardinal for having had the temple "e il Musaico che resta" drawn, though this may refer to the whole mosaic.[41] However, there are fragments of the original which do not appear in the Dal Pozzo copies, and Cardinal Barberini may have had these retrieved from the cellar and re-inserted in the mosaic, then being restored (see below, p. 72). That the Dal Pozzo copies were the basis for the restoration (though the Naples manuscript says only "disegni di casa") is also implied by Carlo Dati in his Orazione delle lodi del Commendatore del Pozzo:[42]

> "... to him is owed the restoration of the mosaic pavement in the temple of Fortune constructed at Praeneste by L. Silla, because a part which was broken up was preserved in his complete drawing of it".

The mosaic remained in position in the Palazzo until 1853, when it was once again taken to Rome, restored by Vatican mosaicists under the direction of Giovanni Azzurri, and returned to Palestrina in 1855.[43] During the Second World War, it was removed from the Palazzo for safety and stored in Rome, and after the war a thorough restoration and examination of the mosaic was undertaken. This time the work served to clarify, rather than further obscure, its history: the tufa backing of the mosaic was stripped off to reveal the reverse side of the tesserae, and the differences between the original, the seventeenth-century and the nineteenth-century patches could clearly be seen from the variation in the thickness of the tesserae and the type of cement used to fix them. The operation has been fully documented, and its relation to the mosaic's previous history discussed in detail, by Salvatore Aurigemma.[44] In the mid-1950s the mosaic was brought back to Palestrina and set on a wall in the Palazzo, now the Museo Nazionale Prenestino, where it may be seen at the present time.

The early documentation of the mosaic is worth examining in some detail because it may help to establish the date of Dal Pozzo's copies. The possibility exists that he did not comission them, but obtained them from someone else who had them executed. The most likely candidate would be Cesi, but if this were the case it is probable that there would be some reference to them as such in Suares' account. To judge by the Cesi document transcribed by Stelluti, quoted above,[45] Cesi did have drawings made ("... pervidere, expingereque....") and these may be the source of the illustrations included by Suares.[46]

The reference in the Cesi account to " Lincaeum collegam nostrum" must date the passage in or post 1622, when Dal Pozzo became a member of the Accademia. Born in Turin in 1588, he was in Rome in 1614 and made the acquaintance of Cesi in 1618, but their close association probably dates from the time of his becoming a *Lynceus*.[47] Cesi died in 1630 (and meetings of the Accademia fell into abeyance after this date), so Dal Pozzo's copies must have existed before this time, if these words are actually Cesi's. They may however be an interpolation of Stelluti's, since the latter could equally well refer to Dal Pozzo as "Lyncaeum collegam nostrum" and might have added this clause as a helpful gloss, in which case the *terminus ante quem* for the drawings could be increased to an outer limit of 1637, the date of Suares' receiving Stelluti's copy of the account. Pieralisi thought that the account was written by Cesi some years after his visit of 1614, and postulated 1624 as a likely date, believing Dal Pozzo's copies to have been made in the interim, "poco dopo 1614".[48] Although this is possible, I think the early date unlikely; the period of Dal Pozzo's activity in collecting drawings may be set at the outside as 1610-1655,[49] but it seems improbable that he would have had copies made of such an important (and, at the time, rather inaccessible) work as the Palestrina mosaic so early in his career, and in any case, if the intermediary between Dal Pozzo and the mosaic was Prince Cesi, then the copies would post 1618 at the earliest.

Where was the mosaic when Dal Pozzo's copies were made? The possibility that it was in situ can almost certainly be ruled out, because the watercolours are of too high a quality to have been executed "accensis facibus, superaffusaque ad perspicuitatem aqua", the unfavourable conditions described in the Cesi-Stelluti account.[50] The copies were probably made in Rome, from the pieces sent there by Cardinal Peretti in 1624-6.[51] Had it been possible to show the mosaic as a whole, Dal Pozzo's artist would probably have done so, but what he has copied are clearly pieces, for they often show a petering-out at the edges which must indicate that what he had before him were damaged fragments. Although several parts join fairly accurately, a few bear no immediate relation to the other pieces, and it is easy to imagine that Peretti had those sections of the mosaic which were in a fairly good condition raised, sometimes cutting them into two or three smaller and more portable blocks, and left behind the more damaged areas. Thus Dal Pozzo's copies would date from some time after 1626, when the mosaic reached Rome. During 1625-6 he was out of Italy, serving on Cardinal Francesco Barberini's legation in France and Spain; he was a member of the Cardinal's household, in the capacity of secretary, thereafter.[52] It may not be too fanciful to suggest that it was the combination of both Cesi's and Barberini's enthusiasm for the mosaic that prompted him to obtain copies of it, the latter's interest in it, witnessed by the Peretti-Magalotti transfer and the eventual restitution to Palestrina, being both antiquarian and proprietorial. It would seem, therefore, that the copies date from some time between the years 1626 to 1630 or 1637, the later date being perhaps the more likely, even though it necessitates supposing an addition of Stelluti's to his copy of Cesi's account.

A closer dating of the copies might be attempted if it were possible to identify the artist. In one source we are told that he was Pietro Testa, who was born in 1607 and was drowned in the Tiber in 1650; as a young man he worked for a time in the studio of Pietro da Cortona. Dal Pozzo seems to have employed him extensively to make copies of antiquities — in his life of Testa, Baldinucci enumerates five large volumes of drawings executed for Cavaliere dal Pozzo by the artist himself ("di sua mano") and gives a brief description of them . Four volumes contain scenes taken from bas-reliefs or drawings of vases, statues and so forth, grouped, according to Dal Pozzo's system, by topic; finally there is the fifth —

> "... in which are to be seen the illustrations of the antique Vergil and of the Vatican Terence, the mosaic from the Temple of Fortune at Palestrina, made by Sulla, and other coloured items ...."[53]

Re-arrangement of the Dal Pozzo portfolios at Windsor (see below, p. 10) has made it difficult to identify each of the groups of drawings mentioned by Baldinucci, and the style of the copies after the antique does not resemble that of Testa's later work, though of course many of them would belong to the early part of his career. Making allowances for a difference in style and technique between Testa's original works and his copies, Sir Anthony Blunt has suggested a large group of the Windsor-Dal Pozzo drawings as the work of this artist, including possibly one set of Vergil drawings;[54] but the attribution of the Palestrina copies is still uncertain, and Baldinucci's evidence cannot be wholeheartedly accepted.[55] The style of the coloured copies of the Vatican Vergil and Terence manuscripts at Windsor is quite unlike that of the Palestrina drawings; nor do the latter particularly resemble the copies of Christian mosaics contained in the two folios labelled "Musaici Antichi", which came to the Royal Library from the Dal Pozzo collection.

The number of Palestrina mosaic copies in Dal Pozzo's possession is recorded by Suares as eighteen, and he gives a brief description of each in the mantissa of his history of Praeneste.[56] His reason for doing so, he says, is because it is more convenient to do this than to attempt a re-assembly of the mosaic, "such as has just been most successfully undertaken at the Prince's palazzo" ("sicut in Palatio Principis iam coeptum est felicissime"), from the drawings. The list shows a quite random order, which probably reflects that of Dal Pozzo's collection, and the descriptions are not always comprehensive or accurate; they give the impression of having been written in something of a hurry, either by Suares himself or by someone in the Barberini household responding in some haste to a request from him. In the absence of the copies themselves this rather sketchy inventory has been a vital element in attempts to reconstruct the mosaic's pre-restoration form, and even with the watercolours to hand it is still of some importance, for there are in fact nineteen copies at Windsor, and one which is missing from Suares' list may have been appended to the collection after the time of his writing.[57] Although most of the mantissa dates to 1652-5, the list probably belongs to the early 1640s, the time of the mosaic's restoration — hence the statement quoted above.[58]

After Dal Pozzo's death in 1657, his great collection of drawings after the antique passed to various members of his family, thence, in about 1703, to the Albani family, and finally, in 1762, a large part of it came into the possession of King George II and entered the Royal Library at Windsor.[59] Dal Pozzo's arrangement was abandoned and the drawings were mostly re-distributed in new portfolios.[60] Exactly which drawings belonged to the Museum Chartaceum it was no longer possible to say, though an attempt to isolate some of the groups was made by Michaelis when he published a list of the contents of the Royal Library in Ancient Marbles in Great Britain.[61] There is no specific mention of the Palestrina watercolours in Michaelis's list, nor in any other of the various notes of drawings of antiquities at Windsor published around this time.[62]

It was the intention of Thomas Ashby to publish a complete catalogue of drawings of antiquities in English collections, a project which was never fully realised. The preliminary notes which Ashby had made on the Windsor collection are preserved with some of his papers in the library of the British School at Rome, and they include some brief observations on the Palestrina copies and the most obvious differences between them and the restored mosaic.[63] The drawings have not been examined in any twentieth-century publication, although their existence at Windsor was noted in Stephan Waetzoldt's study of copies of church mosaics, and five of them appeared as illustrations in Sir Anthony Blunt's work on Poussin in 1967.[64]

II

THE DAL POZZO COPIES

The Palestrina mosaic copies are contained in Windsor Portfolio Pf. Z and bear the numbers 19201-219, replacing an older set of numbers 12055-73.[1] They are executed in ink, the artist having made some preliminary outline strokes in pencil (these are easy to make out where the edge of fragmentary pieces was problematic and no further drawing was done), and filled in with water-colour, the tones employed being rather brighter than those of the actual mosaic. Great care has been taken to indicate the tesserae with grid-like cross-hatching, white against dark colours and brownish-grey against light, and to follow the practice of the original mosaic in outlining figures and objects with a contoured border, generally two tesserae deep. A slightly different technique is employed in no. 11, where dark tesserae have been blocked in, leaving a margin of unpainted paper around to indicate the cement; this may reflect an actual difference in the mosaic, or may be the artist's attempt at finding another way of indicating tesserae. The copies have no uniform scale but vary from two-thirds to one-third life-size approximately. The artist seems to have worked by eye without any measurements; the relative position of objects has sometimes been changed in the final inked-in drawing, but the original draft pencil marks can still be seen under the colouring. In cases where two copies fit together the joins are not quite perfect, and a comparison of unrestored patches of the mosaic and the relevant parts of the watercolours shows minor inaccuracies in the latter's spacing of objects. No. 15 is by a different hand (see below). In addition to this main series, there are at Windsor four other drawings of the mosaic, nos. 11476, 11477, 11483 and 11484 in the large miscellaneous Dal Pozzo folio, Vol. 196, "Nettuno".[2] These are pen-and-ink drawings (with pencilled rough outlines) on similar paper to that of the main set and probably by the same artist. They are rather more sketchy than the coloured series, and look almost like a trial run for it; they are discussed in detail under the corresponding sections, nos. 13 and 15, below.

1. No. 19201 (Fig. 1a). 36 x 31 cm; over one-third life-size.

> (= Suares tab. 4: "In quarta aves, forte Ibides insidentes rupi, quas vorat serpens sinuosa torquens volumina, Simiam, et quadrupedem humana facie, sed caudatam, subtusque ΜΟΝΟΚΕΝΤΑΥΡΑ, tum duo animalia sese lambentia, vel commordentia, additumque ΘΩΑΝΤΕϹ.")[3]

The copy shows as a united whole two pieces which are now placed at opposite ends at the top of the mosaic: the human-headed ΟΝΟΚΕΝΤΑΥΡΑ [4] now finds itself on top of a rocky outcrop in the top right-hand corner, while the lower part of the scene, with the coiled snake and the ΘΩΑΝΤΕϹ forms the lower half of a similar outcrop in the left-hand corner. The discrepancy between the drawing as described by Suares and the present appearance of the mosaic has been noted before,[5] but the conclusion that the mosaic is wrongly restored has not always been accepted. Aurigemma was of the opinion that the copyist working in Rome had incorrectly fitted together two small fragments,[6] but I think that an examination of the two scenes as they now stand will show that the artist, whose drawing shows no obvious sign of a break, made an accurate transcription of a single piece which was subsequently broken on the disastrous return journey to Palestrina and then mistakenly separated in the re-assembly, the restorers perhaps being misled by two similar pieces of rock. In the mosaic, the lowest part of the bush which appears at the left-hand side of the ΟΝΟΚΕΝΤΑΥΡΑ rock can be seen at the left-hand side of the snake's rock, with a well-defined break-line to the left, so the two pieces should really be fitted together. The subject matter of the scene also demands this: the birds fluttering in the bush (in the right-hand part) have been disturbed by the snake at the foot of the rock (in the left-hand part), so the scene makes more sense if the two sections are combined.[7] On either the break-lines can be seen quite clearly (the top of the snake's rock and the bottom of the ΟΝΟΚΕΝΤΑΥΡΑ rock are all restoration) and I think there can be little doubt that they should be joined together as a single unit, just as the Dal Pozzo copy shows. This introduces a problem, because the combined size of the two pieces is greater than that of the left-hand piece in its present form, and would exceed the upper limit of the mosaic as it now is. In addition, the piece is set slightly diagonally, in order to fit into the semicircular outline of the top, but the copy joins the two pieces below in such a way that it would seem to have been set perfectly straight horizontally in the original lay-out of the mosaic. The restorers presumably engineered it at a slant to fit in. The phasing-out at the left of the copy indicates a fragmentary edge which has been padded out in the mosaic with a bush and some anonymous rock.

At the right-hand side the piece joins with no. 2, below.

2. No. 19202 (Fig. 2a). 36.5 x 46 cm with a horizontal join in the paper 17.8 cm from the top; about one-third life-size.

> (= Suares tab. 2: "In secunda cancros innantes Fluvio, Simias, Hippopotamum, venatores, et in his Mauros, qui vibrant sagittas ex arcubus in Simiam, infra ϹΦΙΝΓΙΑ.")

At the top left-hand corner of the watercolour appears the hind leg and tail of one of the ΘΩΑΝΤΕϹ from no. 1, together with the edge of the rock formation. On the rock below stands the animal identified by Suares as "hippopotamum"; it has no inscription in the copy and there is nothing about the area below its feet to suggest that there were tesserae missing and the artist was not sure how to proceed. Yet this space in the restored mosaic contains the fragmentary letters ΞΙΟΙΓ, which do not make any sense. The patch is one which was restored in the seventeenth century,[8] and it may be that the restorers felt that the animal's lack of a label was odd (together with the wild ass in no. 6 it is the only surviving large animal in the upper section of the mosaic to lack an inscription), and decided to supply one, or mistook the fragmentary label of another, vanished animal and placed it here. Alternatively but less likely, the letters really did exist below the creature in the original and the artist skated over the difficulty because he could not make sense of them.[9] The piece of mosaic seems to have been fragmentary at the right-hand side, so that the copyist did not know how to continue the rock formation on which the monkey is sitting. The pool of water which begins below the monkey's foot has disappeared in the mosaic; the patch has been incorporated in the extended rock, which then ends abruptly, the space above being filled in with water and a plant.

At the lower left-hand side the section joins with no. 4, below.

3. No. 19203 (Fig. 3a). 45 x 34.5 cm; a little under half life-size.

(= Suares tab. 14: "ΚΡΟΚΟΤΑϹ [sic], venatores, ΥΑΒΟΥϹ in rupe ad Fluvium.")

The contours of the fragment shown by the copy can still be traced on the mosaic - the break above the rock is quite apparent in the sudden change of the tesserae, and that at the base, which leaves the ΝΑΒΟΥϹ (mistakenly read as ΥΑΒΟΥϹ by Suares) without any feet, has not been remedied: almost the whole of the animal, and the top of the rock below, is restored, the latter rather improbably blocking the space where one might expect to see the beast's feet.[10] Perhaps the restorer was uncertain of what sort of feet it might have and thought this the easiest way round the problem. On top of the rock in the copy are two pairs of vertical lines, drawn in ink but not painted. They look rather like birds' legs. The fragment came to an end at this point, and the artist was not sure what to make of this detail, nor of the right-hand side of the scene. A line intersects the right-hand wing of the bird in flight and below this is a patch of dark-green paint outlined with magenta and not squared off; then a gap, then what is apparently rock - but the artist has tentatively sketched in an elephant The mosaic must have been so fragmentary at this point that he was uncertain whether to see an animal there or not.[11] Further down, behind the head of the ΝΑΒΟΥϹ , is a patch of pale blue (?water), not tessellated, and at the bottom a gap. Another gap, at the bottom left-hand corner, is lined-off as if a piece of rock occupied the space. In the restored mosaic the right-hand side of the scene has been abruptly finished off against a background of sky, though traces of the green patch below the bird and the strange rocks below can still be seen and are original.[12] 19203 makes no apparent join with any other piece.

4. No. 19204 (Fig. 4a). 46.5 x 22.8 cm; about half life-size.

(= Suares tab. 3: "In tertia Testudines innatantes Fluvio, et feras quae devorant pisces, inscriptumque ΕΝΥΔΡΙϹ .")

19204 seems to join no. 2 at the right-hand side (the end of the rock on which the ΞΙΟΙΓ animal stands - a gap should possibly be allowed) and no. 1 at the top (the disturbance in the water within the patch of weeds at the top is probably caused by a projecting piece of rock above[13] and the two ink lines to the left carry on in the same plane as the ground lines below the snake). The three pieces thus make up a single block of the original mosaic. The copy shows one slight deviation from the scene as it now appears in the mosaic: below the rock on which the turtles clamber is a strip of land extending to the left. In the mosaic, the turtles' rock finishes abruptly and a spit of land is seen below but further left, with grass along its edge.[14] Although the copyist may have mistakenly placed the land too near the rock, some change seems to have occurred in restoration, the original land being omitted and replaced with this more distant patch. At the bottom left-hand corner of the drawing the figure "2" has been written.

5. No. 19205 (Fig. 5a). 25.7 x 29 cm; over half life-size.

> (= Suares tab. 1: "In prima Tabula spectare datur tres feras a Musivo compositas, quibus inscriptum ΥΛΜΟΝΟΠΑΡΔΑΛΙ forte ΚΑΜΕΛΟΠΑΡΔΑΛΙ.")

The fragment here shown may join to no. 6 at the right-hand side (see below) but does not relate to any others. The background in the top left-hand corner of the copy seems to be sky, not water as is now the case in the mosaic; it is coloured plain, pale grey-blue.[15] It would seem that the piece really belongs in the sky-line register of the mosaic, and its present position is incorrect. In addition, there should perhaps be a tree at the left, since the left-hand giraffe is craning up to eat some foliage of which only the periphery is indicated by scattered green tesserae, though he is presumably feeding on a tree or bush like that into which the right-hand giraffe is poking its head. The copy shows slightly more of the inscription below the giraffes than has been preserved in the mosaic: Κ'ΜΕΛΟ .ΠΑΡΔΑΛ! as opposed to Κ ΜΛΟ ΙΑΡΔΑΛΙ.[16]

6. No. 19206 (Fig. 6a). 48.8 x 34.4 cm; under half life-size.

> (= Suares tab. 12: "In XII legitur ΚΗΙΥΙΤΗΝ ΛΕΑΙΝΑ CΑΥΟC ΤCΗΧΙCΝΙΕ ΕΦΑΛΟC.")[17]

The artist has copied a section of the mosaic which became fragmentary at the right-hand side, where, at the top, he has drawn but not coloured in a shape reminiscent of an elephant whose tusks intersect a patch of blue ?sky, to the left of which is purplish-brown rock. Had there originally been an animal in this position it would conveniently fill the lacuna now occupied by a pool of water (all restoration).[18] At the top the rock has been finished off abruptly in the mosaic to block the space where the feet of the ΝΑΒΟΥC might appear (cf. above), but the drawing suggests that it in fact extended some way further up. Below the elephant shape at the right, the artist has painted but not squared-in the continuation of the rock formation: two dark-green lines enclosing an area of pinkish-brown. This is continued at the left-hand side of the following piece, no. 7, and the dark-blue inlet which begins above the inscription ΑΓΕΛΑΡΥ at the lower right-hand side is similarly continued, after a gap, on no. 7. The space between must have been occupied by the animal thus labelled, ΑΓΕΛΑΡΥ being merely the beginning of the word, which may be ΑΓΕΛΑΡΧΟC.[19] No inscription now exists for the wild ass above the ΛΥΝΞ but one may have been present in the space to the right or in the blank patch below its feet, which is all restoration.

At the upper left-hand side, the piece probably joins with no. 5, as suggested above, but a gap between the two should be envisaged to accommodate the main part of the tree on which the giraffe is feeding in no. 5 and the monkey standing in this piece. The latter's label, ΚΗΠΤΙΕΝ, [20] appears in the copy against a background of darker tesserae which seem to have disappeared in the restored mosaic. At the bottom of the left-hand side, the inscription ΕΦΛΛΟC in the corner may belong to an animal which occupied a space to the left and possibly stood on a rock formation, parts of which can be seen behind the letters ΕΦΛ on this watercolour (coloured green, fading to yellow at the edge), and at the top right-hand corner of no. 10, above the wild boar's back. The area of the restored mosaic shows a rather untidy finishing-off of the rock and a fill-in of water and vague land between the ΧΟΙΡΟΠΙΘΓΙΑ and the two boars. The insertion of the ΕΦΛΛΟC animal would necessitate an increase in the space between these two areas which would correspond to that apparently necessary to accommodate the tree, and also the larger gap between nos. 9 and 10 below. [21]

7. No. 19207 (Fig. 7a). 57.2 x 34.5 cm with a vertical join 11 cm from the left; a little under half life-size.

(= Suares tab. 15: "In XV ΤΙΓΡΙC ΚΡΟΚΟΔΙΛΟC ΧΕΡCΑΙΟC CΑΤΤΙΟΚ.") [22]

As noted above, the left-hand side of the scene seems to connect with the right-hand side of no. 6, since the pinkish-brown strip outlined in dark-green continues here, below the ΑΡΚΟC. Below this is a space with the number "4" written in the top right-hand corner. This corresponds to a similar space at the top left of no. 11, in which the artist has again written "4". The gap might have been occupied in the original by the ΑΓΕΛΑΡΥ animal of no. 6; in the restored mosaic it has been filled in with water and rocks. Several horizontal pencil strokes suggest that the artist tried to see how the two pieces linked up. At the top of the copy, the patch to the left, above the head of the bear and the rock to its right, is pale-blue open sky, so the present location of this piece in the mosaic (water behind the bear, and more rock again above the piece shown in the copy) seems incorrect: it should be up at the sky-line. (A small area of sky still appears above the snake coiling around the rock, with the restored mass of rock at the left.)

At the right of the copy, the monkey sitting on the rock is labelled CΑΤΤΥΟC but this section was presumably damaged on the journey back to Palestrina and the inscription lost, for it no longer appears in the mosaic. The fragment tails off at the right-hand side with heavy shadowing at the side of the rock but the restorers have continued both the rock, together with the smaller formation behind the CΑΤΤΥΟC which comes to a clearly-defined end in the drawing, and the tree above, which the copy shows as ending above the dark shadowing, in order to fill the space between this section and the outer limit of the mosaic. [23] The top branch of the tree has been put in, but the shoot coming off at the right ignored. Along the lower edge, this piece joins no. 11 (see below).

8. No. 19208 (Fig. 8a). 44.7 x 22.5 cm; approximately one-third life-size.

(= Suares tab. 9: "In nona Templum ad ripam Fluvii, Obelisci, puteus, palma, mulieres vero sertis coronatae, homo tridentifer forte Neptunus.")

The copy corresponds closely with this part of the mosaic, one of the least restored areas. The right-hand side terminates with a straight edge which interesects the tower behind the temple, but the side view of the tower and the top left-hand part of the tower below in the mosaic are original. Since they do not appear in the copy, they may be among the fragments collected and incorporated into the mosaic at the time of re-assembly.[24] In the absence of the side view of the tower in the piece he was copying, the artist has inserted a narrow perspective view at the left of the tower, above the temple roof. The bottom left-hand side of the copy indicates a fragmentary edge, with a dark-green plant beside the well, and a patch of plain green to the left of it. This has been amplified in the mosaic to form a dense bush to the left of the well, and plain ground beyond.

Since this part of the mosaic is almost entirely original, it is interesting to note the tonal variations between the mosaic and the copy: the artist has shown the side of the temple in uniformly dark shadow, and the narrow view of the interior which appears between the portico and the pilaster in lighter shadow. The reverse is true of the mosaic, which shows the latter view in heavy shadow, and the side view of the temple in light-grey shadow with a few dark splotches - these are ignored by the artist. The piece joins no. 12 along the lower edge, though the two watercolours do not fit together perfectly.

9. No. 19209 (Fig. 9a). 48.4 x 33 cm; almost half life-size.

> (= Suares tab. 10: "In decima ΡΙΝΟΚΕΡΩC, ΧΟΙΡΟΠΙΟΚ, Templum cum duabus turribus, et casa, palmae.")

The copy shows the small reed shelter (bottom right-hand corner) with a single doorway and a fence (?) between it and the tower to the left; to the right is a space above which some foliage has been sketched. In the mosaic, however, the hut has been restored with two openings, the detail of the fence partly lost, and the space to the right occupied by a tree. Directly above this space the watercolour is the tapering end of the spit of land on which the ΧΟΙΡΟΠΙΘΙΛ stands, but this comes to an abrupt halt in the mosaic, the small gap between this animal and the boars being filled with amorphous land.[25] At the left-hand side of the copy the rock on which the ΡΙΝΟΚΕΡΩC stands also seems to taper off, but is now blocked at the left in the mosaic by another rock. At the bottom of the copy the artist has drawn in some lines where the walls of the temple and tower complex peter out, probably to indicate the edge of the fragment.

10. No. 19210 (Fig. 10a). 47 x 28.8 cm; approximately one-third life-size.

> (= Suares tab. 8: "In octava navis inflato velo tendit ad turrim rotundam, et ad duas quadratas in mare procurrentes, in quibus nidificunt volucres, sagittarius collineans in Hippopotamum.")

The pieces shown in nos. 9 and 10 have been placed side by side in the restored mosaic, presumably because the foliage which appears at the right of 9 might belong to the tree at the left-hand side of 10. This is however no more than a tentative location, and even if the sections were to be placed adjacent to each other, the space between them would need to be increased in order to accommodate the spit of land and the gap between the hut and the tree in no. 9, and to allow the fore-part of the boar whose back legs appear here to be depicted in a rather less cramped fashion than is now employed in the mosaic. The additional space would also permit a better termination for the ground on which the boars stand and possibly an inscription for them. At the left-hand side of the lower edge, directly below the small reed hut, is a patch of roughly sketched vegetation which now appears, somewhat improbably, on top of the tower below.[26] The section in which the latter is shown (see no. 13, below) may well be in the wrong place.

Along the upper edge the piece joins no. 6, probably with a slight gap in between them; at the right-hand side it joins no. 11, below.

11. No. 19211 (Fig. 11a). 57.7 x 35.2 cm with an L-shaped join at the left, 10.7 cm across at the top and 21 cm at the bottom; almost half life-size.

> (= Suares tab. 7: "In septima ΚΡΟΚΟΔΙΛΟΠΑΡΔΑΛΙC innat Flumini, hanc agitant Aethiopes clypeati, aedes, simulacra Isidis, Aquilae signum Asino impositum.")

At the left of the scene is the stern of the boat which appears in no. 10; the two copies do not quite join perfectly. Above is a space which corresponds to that on no. 7 and is likewise labelled "4". If, as suggested above, this gap was originally occupied by an animal, this would supply an object for the Ethiopian hunters to the right who are looking and gesticulating at something in that area. The copy peters out at the right-hand side, as does no. 7, and the restorers have finished off the platform on which the temple stands, extended the rock above and filled in with water elsewhere.

The watercolour shows that the form of the temple has been altered slightly in restoration. The wall directly behind the first tower at the left is pierced below its four windows by a long slit which gives a view through to the water behind, shown as vivid blue: but the restorer has taken this slit as a space between the tower at the front and this wall behind, making the left-hand half of the wall the side of the tower in front, seen in perspective. Some change has also occurred within the group of hunters above: in the copy the first hunter at the left stands directly above the wall with the slit in it and his right arm, which is bent double at the elbow (a view the artist has tried to clarify by painting the forearm lighter), is immediately adjacent to the shield of the next hunter. In the mosaic, however, he appears above the tower to the left of the wall and there is a gap between him and the other figure; his right arm now has the addition of a hand, perhaps because the restorers found the view of it doubled ambiguous. At the bottom left-hand corner of the copy the figure on foot behind the rider is carrying a bundle on a stick, and behind him appears the rudder of the boat, manipulated by a shadowy figure sitting in the stern. The restorers have given the figure a flying cloak in place of his bundle, and the detail of the rudder has been lost.

Where the paper has been joined at the left-hand side of the watercolour, differences of execution can be seen in the two sections. The join has not been made with complete accuracy - for example, the two versions of the cornice at the top of the pylon tower do not fit. The left-hand piece is rather less neat, and the outlines are not drawn in ink as elsewhere but painted in black; in addition there is a slight difference in the colours, and in the lower part of the copy the tesserae have not been marked. The difference between the ink and paint outlines indicates that the artist first made the drawings in ink and then coloured them in when he had completed the whole set; presumably he ran out of paper for this one and did not finish it until he was working on the colouring. The technique of blocking-in the tesserae (cf. p. 11) appears several times here, for example: in the extreme right-hand doorway of the temple, in the shadowed patch of wall above and to left of it and in the back left-hand tower.

12. No. 19212 (Fig. 12a). 48.3 x 21.3 cm; about one-third life-size.

> (= Suares tab. 5: "Quinta exhibet phaselum, qui remis agitur in Flumine rupibus interstincto, in quo milites, qui iacula conijiciunt in Hippopotamum, quibus illum inter ulvas, seu Papyros configunt.")

This section joins along the upper edge to no. 8 and along the lower to no. 18. It shows no variations on the scene as it now appears in the mosaic, save that the copy preserves slightly more of the left-hand side: the nose of the hippopotamus and the end of the strip of land on which he is standing.

13. No. 19213 (Fig. 13a). 81 x 61 cm with a vertical join 44.5 cm from the left; half life-size.

> (= Suares tab. 16: "XV[I] tentorium, et milites, atque Templum, Dux propinans cum cornu, Abacus, Fluvius.")

This is the largest piece copied, and the artist has used two sheets of paper, the join between which is clearly visible at the point where the soldiers' shields are piled up below the awning. The two pieces have not been fitted together quite accurately - notice, for instance, the discrepancies of matching up the lines on the awning, the abrupt end of the outline of the left-hand tree above, or the column below the awning, which is a little too narrow. The shoulder and arm of the soldier standing in front of this column are missing, and the pile of helmets and shields below is rather muddled and has not been coloured in. The level of the bottom of the right-hand piece is higher than that of the left. As I have mentioned earlier (p. 11), there are at Windsor four pen-and-ink drawings of the mosaic in addition to the coloured set, and three of these show parts of the scene which appears here: no. 11476 shows part of the awning, the roof of the temple and the trees above; no. 11477, the top left-hand section of the scene with the walled complex, the man punting a papyrus boat and part of the tower to the right of him; and no. 11483, the left-hand side of the temple, finishing at the left just beyond the <u>cratera</u> and at the right at the same point as the division in the two sections of the watercolour. I have suggested that the sketches, which are rather summarily executed, are the work of the same artist as the main set of drawings, and may represent his first attempt at copying the mosaic. The size of the drawings is rather larger than that of the corresponding sections of no. 13, so he may have begun with these larger sketches, the scale of which is approaching life-size, but decided that they were too unwieldy when fitted together and so abandoned them and opted for a smaller format. 11476 and 11477 show no variations from the details appearing in no. 13, but 11483 (Fig. 13c) has some small but significant differences at the right-hand side: the soldier's arm and shoulder which have disappeared at the join in the watercolour are present here in front of the column, his outstretched arm holding a spear. The helmet and shield at the bottom of the pile below the column actually belong to a figure in the sketch, seen with face three-quarters turned away and back to the spectator,[27] while the figure in a tunic seen in profile above and to the right is bearded in the sketch but not in the watercolour. Whether the fact that the artist made three separate sketches indicates that the scene was in at least three pieces is impossible to say for sure, though it seems unlikely. He may have been experimenting to find a suitable scale and could not fit more than about a quarter of the scene at the larger scale on the paper he had to hand. It is not so clear, however, that the vertical join in no. 13 does not reflect an actual division in the fragment, because here there is some confusion at the joining edges which might be attributable to missing patches in the mosaic. The divergence in detail between 11483 and the corresponding area of no. 13 could be a mistake on the part of the artist, perhaps sketching 11483 more hurriedly, or it could represent two attempts at interpreting a damaged area of mosaic. No. 13 may be made up from two separate copies which the artist subsequently joined because the two pieces of mosaic obviously fitted together.[28]

The most notable difference between the copy and the mosaic (which is heavily restored in this part) lies in the figure of the woman, usually taken for a priestess, standing at the right. In the drawing, she has no object in her upraised right hand, but in the mosaic she holds a simpulum. Most of her arm, and the simpulum, belong to a patch of the mosaic which is original, so a mistake on the part of the artist must be assumed.[29] The fragment does not seem to relate to any of those which now surround it, but apparently joins at the right-hand side no. 14, a piece which is not present in the restored mosaic.

At the top left-hand corner is the lower half of a walled enclosure with a tower at the right, only the base of which is visible. This seems to have been restored over-simply in the mosaic, with the top of the tower put in (ignoring the dark patch to the left, which is really the side view of the wall, but is made part of the tower in the mosaic),[30] and the wall merely terminated at the other end. There should probably be a tower here, too, to judge by a similar enclosure above and to the left, and also by the fact that at the edge of the copy the crenellations seem to break off and there is a gap which may indicate the beginning of a wall or building. At the bottom right-hand corner of the scene, the ground below the female figure seems to have been altered slightly in restoration, the dark strip at the edge and the plant to the left having disappeared.

14. No. 19214 (Fig. 14). 48.3 x 28.5 cm.

(= Suares tab. 18: "Umbella.")[31]

19214 shows a part of the mosaic which, if it does belong, was either lost or thrown away, as being too damaged or too difficult to fit in, before the mosaic was re-assembled. The manner in which the artist has drawn it suggests that it was a small fragment which he felt ought to link up with 19213 but he could not see exactly how. At the left of the copy he has sketched in ink the upper half of the female figure (still without simpulum, cf. above) and her palm branch, the palm-like plant to the right,[32] the tip of the horn held by the soldier, and behind this two lines which probably indicate the column; to the left of this he has begun to sketch a figure which does not appear in the scene.[33] Above and to right of the female figure, who is set at a slightly different angle from that at which she appears in no. 13, is the pilaster at the back of the temple,[34] and adjoining it is the fragment itself, drawn and coloured in the usual way. At the top right and left the artist has sketched in pencil the contours of the fragment; the lines are faintly visible on either side of the coloured section with the two pairs of feet. The latter stand on a platform or jetty, the left pair belonging to someone whose lower half is clad in a long white garment. Below is an expanse of deep green (?water), against which is a red sunshade with golden fringe, supported by a pole and casting a dark-brown shadow. A similar dark-brown patch, intersected by two white lines, appears to the right, and the copy finishes at this point. At the left-hand side the scene follows a straight line down the side of the presumed pilaster, then appears a patch of dark-brown like two steps in profile, below which is a patch of lighter brown, to the left of which three pairs of lines have been inked-in. The upper of the two steps can still be seen in the mosaic in an unrestored patch, but the space which this scene would occupy (and there is no reason to suppose that it does not belong to the mosaic) has been filled in with plain wall above and boats below, the latter being part of the original mosaic but probably misplaced here (see below, p. 22). Further up is a gateway in the wall which does not appear on any of the drawings but is original:[35] it may be one of the pieces which Cardinal Barberini had collected from the Bishop's Palace before the mosaic's restoration. Above this is a procession of priests passing through a kiosk. They have long white kilts and bare feet, and are walking along a sort of causeway. It seems likely that the figures in no. 14 are also priests, similarly dressed, and the ground under their feet is the continuation of the causeway. The piece thus fits in quite easily as regards subject matter; but even if it survived the return journey to Palestrina, or had not already been discarded in Rome, it would clearly have presented a problem to the restorers, who would not have known what object to supply beneath the sunshade. Since this is obviously an important detail, they may have felt that it was better to scrap the difficult fragment entirely, fill in a corresponding amount of space with innocuous wall and proceed with the rest of the scene as it seemed to fit together.

15. No. 19215 (Fig. 15a). 54.5 x 42.3 cm; with a join 22 cm from the left; two-thirds life-size.

No. 19215 is by a different artist, who shows a less careful approach. The copy, which is made to a larger scale than most of the others and on different paper, is more summarily executed, the tesserae are indicated somewhat roughly, and the range of colours employed is duller. The piece does not feature in Suares' list, so this drawing must post-date the inventory, which probably belongs to the early 1640's (see p. 10). The fragment of mosaic, however, must have been visible before this and cannot have been one of those possibly collected from the original site at the time of restoration, for it appears in drawing no. 11484 (Fig. 15c) of the set of four pen-and-ink drawings mentioned previously. Since these are apparently by the same artist as the coloured set (cf. p. 11) the piece shown in no. 15 must have been with the others at the time of their being drawn, probably in Rome, and the reason for its not being copied then and coloured in as they were is quite inexplicable. At any rate, the omission was noticed and made good at a later date, very likely around the time of the mosaic's restoration, by a different copyist. The scenes shown in 11484 and no. 15 are not identical: the former finishes slightly higher, with the prow and upper part of the man in the papyrus boat at the bottom right-hand corner of the piece, but includes more at the top - the left-hand side of the top of the reed hut, and to left of this a small coracle-like boat (similar to that in the bottom right-hand corner of no. 17) and a section of the stern or prow of a larger boat. These details could have been lost from the edge of the fragment, particularly if the sketch was made before the pieces were taken back to Palestrina and damaged en route. The drawing bears no obvious relation to any other section of the mosaic and may well be misplaced in its present position, where the restorers have inserted it without much additional work - the missing part at the lower right-hand side of the hut's outline, for example, has been left just as it is, with the ragged ends trailing off into thin air. If the evidence of 11484 can be accepted and there were originally boats at the top left-hand side, it could not occupy its present situation exactly as it is since the land above takes up the space where these would appear.

16. No. 19216 (Fig. 16a). 48 x 33.2 cm; over half life-size.

> (= Suares tab. 17: "In XVII Sacerdotum processus sub templo, quatuor coronati gestant humeris fercula, cum tympanis, tibijsque alii, Anubis statua in Base.")

A comparison of the copy and this part of the mosaic (Fig. 16b) shows two important variations in the party of priests who form the central element of the scene. The figure of the fourth priest, whose head is obscured by the ferculum which they are carrying, has been omitted from the mosaic, though sense demands that he should be there to hold the carrying-pole; and a candelabrum-shaped object has been placed on top of the ferculum, though no object appears here in the copy. It is possible that the artist has made a mistake on the lines of the omission of the simpulum in no. 13, since there is a vertical line of light-brown tesserae in the centre of the dark-brown column above the candelabrum which is original but is not indicated by the artist.[36] The candelabrum itself belongs to a patch which is entirely restoration and the light-coloured strip above has been joined on to the top of it. In the original it may have been just a highlight of the column which the artist ignored (cf. his simplification of the shading of the side of the temple in no. 8); or there may have been an object there which he omitted by oversight or because he could not understand it. Whether it would have been a candelabrum is impossible to say: the ferculum is strikingly similar to the bronze base in the form of a small naos decorated with Egyptianising figures and pseudo-hieroglyphs, found at Herculaneum and now in Naples.[37] The base is apparently unique. The decoration runs around the sides but not over the top,[38] so it seems likely that something stood on it - perhaps a fairly light cult object, as has been suggested by Tran tam Tinh in his publication of the Isiac material from Herculaneum.[39]

Apart from these major differences, the copy shows the statue of Anubis to the right of the kiosk a little below the level of the latter, with a plant to the left of it. In the mosaic it has been restored at the same level as the kiosk, and the plant has disappeared. To the right of the statue base are two frond-like plants which have likewise vanished. The copy comes to an abrupt end at the right-hand side, but as the faces of several of the figures are turned towards something happening further right, it seems unlikely that the mosaic originally ended at this point; the restorers have padded out the right-hand side with plain ground in order to fill the space between the figures and the outer edge of the mosaic.

17. No. 19217 (Fig. 17a). 47.5 x 30.5 cm; under half life-size.

> (= Suares tab. 13: "In XIII navis visitur, quae remis agebatur, militibus plena, aliae velis vento inflatis, et funibus intertextis, phaselus in Fluvio, domus, et Casa cum rusticis, cymba, flores in Fluvio.")

The sections of the mosaic shown in nos. 16 and 17 are placed one above the other, but this join may not be correct. At the top of the copy, to the left of the palm tree, is the corner of a platform projecting into the water, and this is intersected by the top of the rigging of the boat below, which is set almost straight horizontally. In the mosaic, however, it has been placed diagonally, in order to fit in with the piece above, and the projecting mass has disappeared. That the placing of the boat is wrong can be seen from the fact that the lines on the water are also diagonal, i.e. the whole piece of mosaic has been manoeuvred to fit. Parts of the boat which have been restored have lost the detail shown in the copy: the ropes of the rigging fore and aft, and the exact form of the cabin, which has been given a ridge roof (the copy seems to show a rounded one, as on the cabin-boat in no. 12) and a perspective view of the short side at the right, while the lattice work has been brought right up to the roof. Further down in the scene, the prow of the warship has been somewhat mangled in restoration[40] so that the object in the right hand of the standing figure, a long trumpet, has disappeared, as have the ends of the two spears in his left hand, and the lotus flower to the left of the prow has turned into a strange object floating in the opposite direction. At the bottom of the piece is foliage which seems to belong to a palm tree rather than a plant and may indicate that originally there was another scene below no. 17. At the right-hand side of the copy, behind and above the small square tower is greenery; this has been brought to a halt in the mosaic, but looks in the watercolour as if it would have continued to the right.

18. No. 19218 (Fig. 18a). 47.4 x 29 cm; half life-size.

> (= Suares tab. 16: "Sexta Hippopotamum telis confixum natantem, duosque Crocodilos.")

The copy joins no. 12 at the upper edge: at the top of the watercolour may be seen the end of the boat's reflection and the tips of the three oar blades from the scene above. This section of the mosaic is one of the least restored parts,[41] and the copy shows no differences. To the right of the nose of the lower crocodile a pair of crossed sticks or stems has been drawn but subsequently coloured over: they correspond to the forked leaves which appear a fraction higher up in the mosaic (in a restored patch).

19. No. 19219 (Fig. 19a). 48 x 37.4 cm; approximately half life-size.

> (= Suares tab. 11: "In undecima vir mulierque hinc discumbunt, inde alii sub tegete, quam inumbrat vitis pampinis, et racemis onusta ad ripam Fluvij, per quem discurrit phaselus plenus floribus innascentibus, ex adverso tres, quorum alius canit fistula, porrigit alter cornu, seu cyathum, qui desinit in hodie speciem, tertius indicem attollit.")

The copy shows a piece of the mosaic which was the subject of much controversy until the twentieth-century restoration, for an almost identical fragment exists in the Berlin Museum (Fig. 19b), and which piece was the original and which the copy was a question disputed by many of those writing about the Palestrina mosaic. Most authors settled in favour of the Palestrina piece as the genuine article, not a little because they wished to preserve the theory of the mosaic's integrity. In spite of the evidence of the Dal Pozzo note published by Lumbroso in 1875 - "Cardinal Magalotto.......having kept for himself a single piece, which he gave to the Grand Duke..." [42] the question was not settled until the post-war work demonstrated that this section of the mosaic was entirely seventeenth-century restoration, so in all likelihood the Berlin piece was the original.[43]

Briefly, the history of the Berlin piece is that it passed from Magalotti via the Grand Duke of Tuscany to Francesco Maria de'Medici, and from him to Pietro Giovanni de' Chiari. In July 1743, Francesco Gori saw it on sale in the market in Florence and, as he succinctly commented, "Ut vidi, obstupui, statimque emi".[44] From Gori it passed to the Margrave of Baireuth, thence to the Berlin Museum; it is now in the Antiken-Sammlung of the Staatliche Museen. It was published in 1875 by Engelmann, who concluded from its quality and colouring that it was a piece of genuinely antique mosaic.[45]

The note published by Lumbroso states that the piece was copied by Calandra from "una copia...a olio esattissima" which was in the Barberini household;[46] this may or may not be one of Dal Pozzo's copies and indeed the Dal Pozzo watercolour may be a copy of the copy. Cardinal Barberini, in his anxiety to secure the mosaic which belonged to the family's new property, was probably reluctant to allow one piece to be detached from the set, but may have found it politic to do so in order to ensure the success of negotiations for the rest; he would quite likely have ordered a copy of the missing section to be made if there was no drawing already in existence. There is nothing about the Dal Pozzo copy to suggest that it was not made contemporaneously with the others, and if it was taken from the original piece of mosaic then it must have been executed while the pieces were with Magalotti (i.e. some time during the years 1629-1637 approximately).

The copied piece has not been altogether successfully fitted into the mosaic. From the photograph of the reverse side published by Aurigemma[47] it can be seen that the copy was made following the lines of the piece as it appears in the watercolour, and then inserted into the mosaic with a good deal of padding-out around. The left-hand side of the pergola has been extended but still ends abruptly, while the top has been finished off with some leaves, and the right-hand side of the scene, with the beginnings of a building of some sort, has been left as it is, with the masonry as an improbable ruin (Fig. 19c). Missing altogether is the strange metallic object, egg-shaped with two longitudinal slits above a semi-circular one and seemingly extended on a rod which just appears at the top between the frame of the pergola and the masonry: this part of the restored mosaic is merely splotchy yellow/brown vegetation. At the bottom of the drawing is a strip of land (below the man punting along in a papyrus boat) which has vanished altogether, and the scene now ends slightly higher up.

From the illustration, Fig 19b, it can be seen that the Gori/Berlin fragment lost some of its perimeter in the course of changing hands, notably in the left-hand corners top and bottom and the top right-hand corner, and has been filled out with restoration to make a straight-sided piece. In most details it corresponds closely with the Dal Pozzo copy and is a valuable indicator of the artist's accuracy.[48] Even less of the metallic object appears than in the watercolour, and it is difficult to imagine what it represents. If Calandra was in fact working from the Dal Pozzo copy, then clearly he could make nothing of this enigmatic object either, and so fudged the part with some nondescript foliage. It seems likely that the tower behind (or whatever it is that the courses of masonry form) did extend some way further up, and also that there should be more surrounding greenery: the dense foliage around the pergola would not have ended as abruptly as it now does in the mosaic. On three sides of the piece, then, there was probably some surrounding scenery which has now disappeared, and its current setting is incorrect.

In two places in the copy a word has been pencilled in, apparently before the colour was applied. These are extremely faint and hard to decipher: at the right-hand side, above the fence and with a line pointing to it "steccato"(?); and an illegible word at the left-hand side, above the lowest bunch of grapes on the pergola.

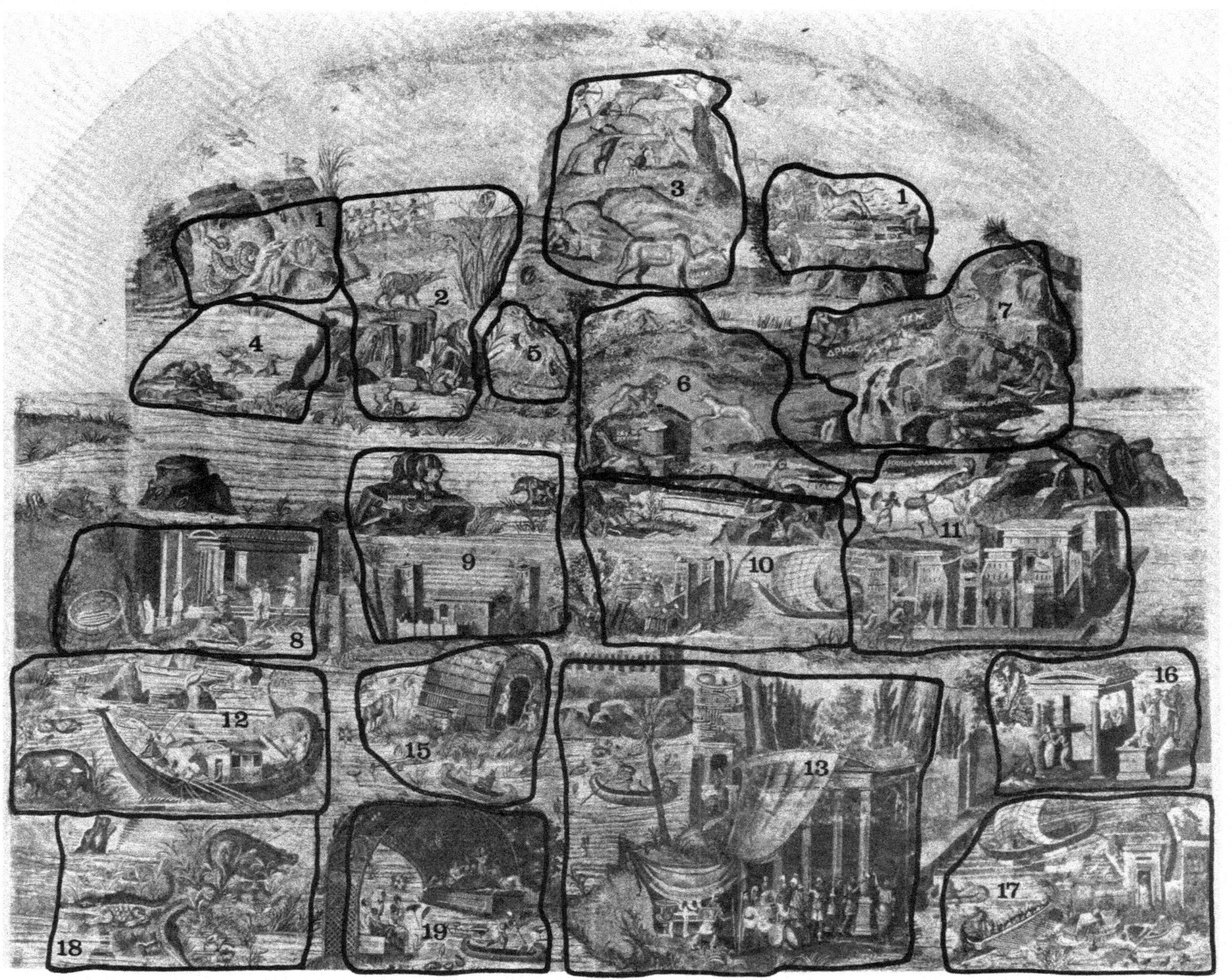

B. The mosaic divided into sections to correspond with the copies

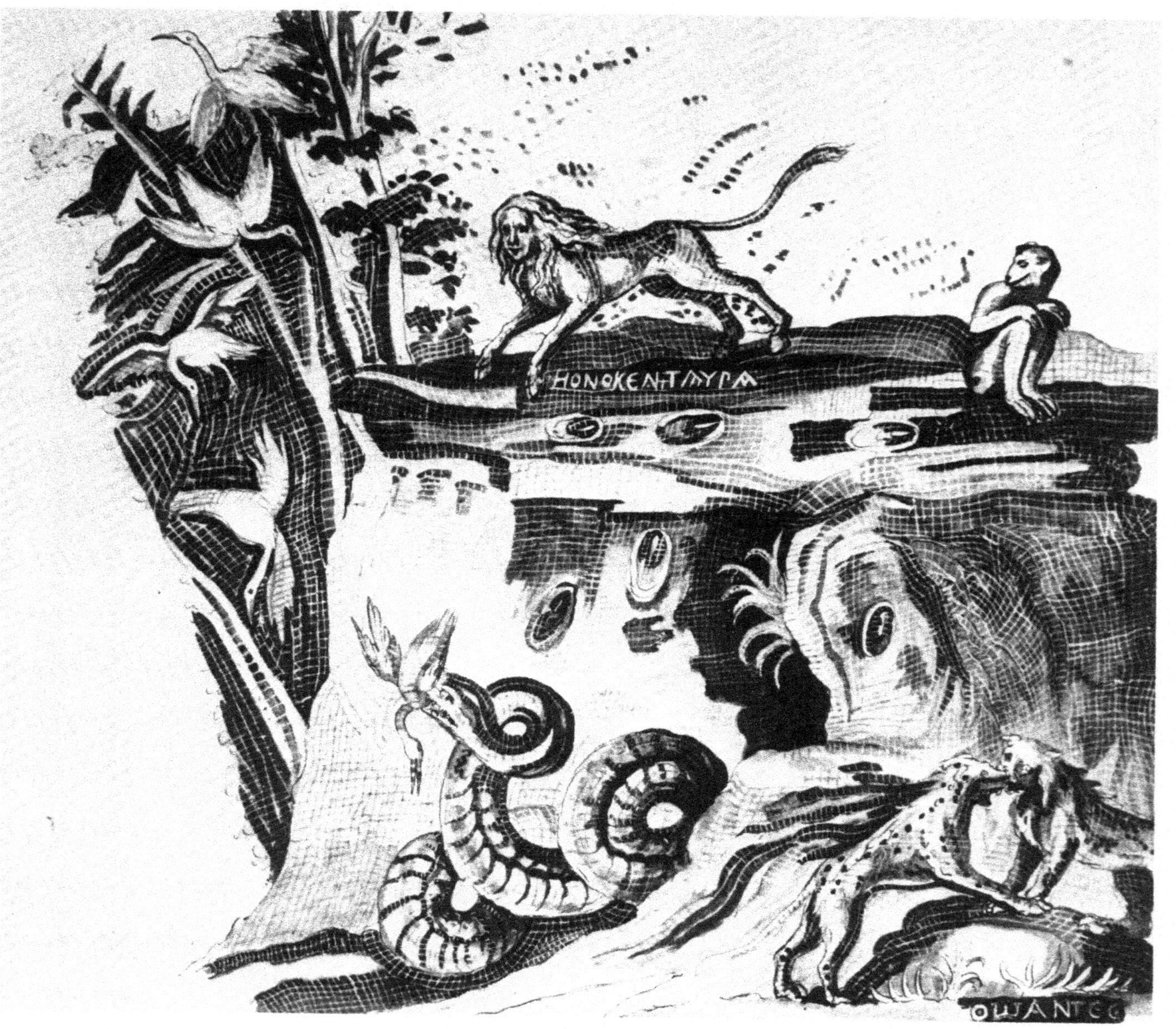

1a.

Windsor drawing 19201

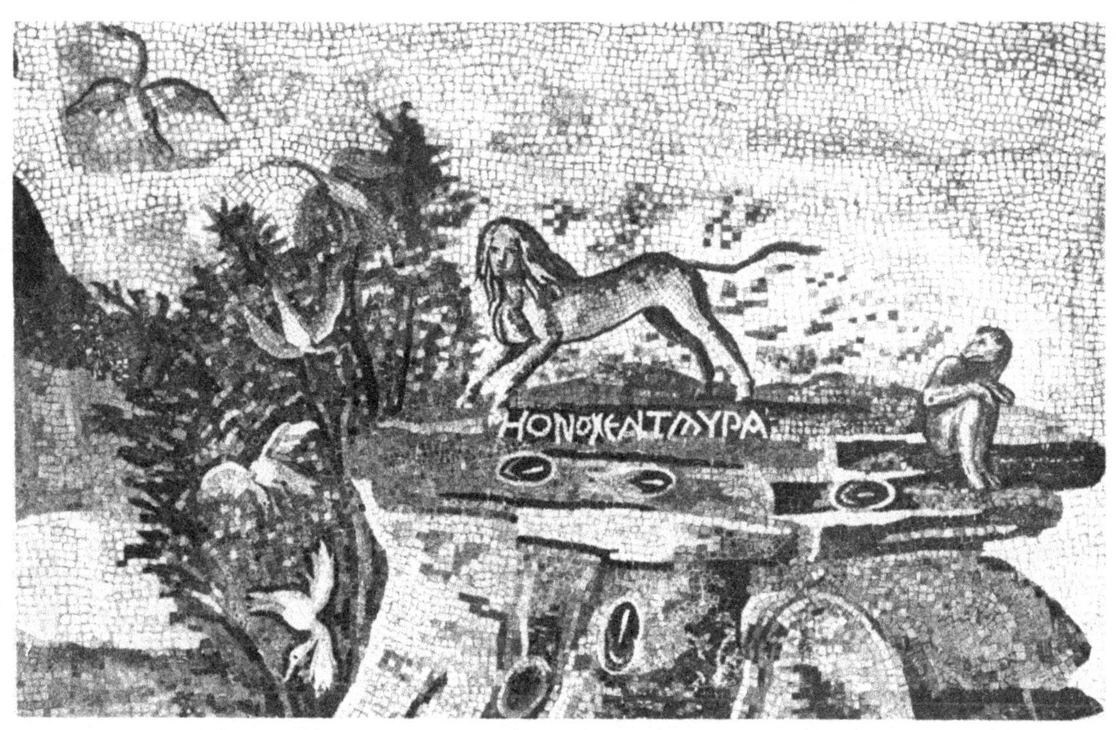

1b. The mosaic, section 1 (right-hand)

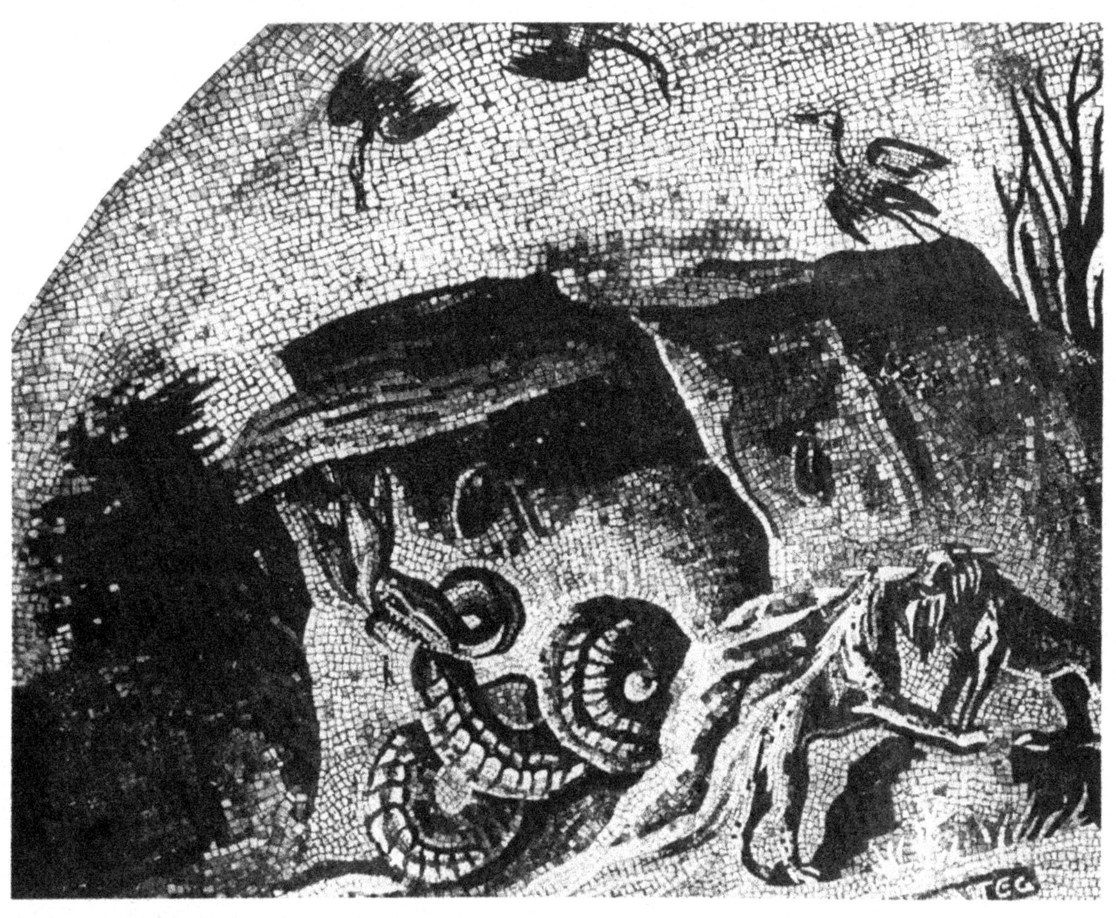

1c. The mosaic, section 1 (left-hand)

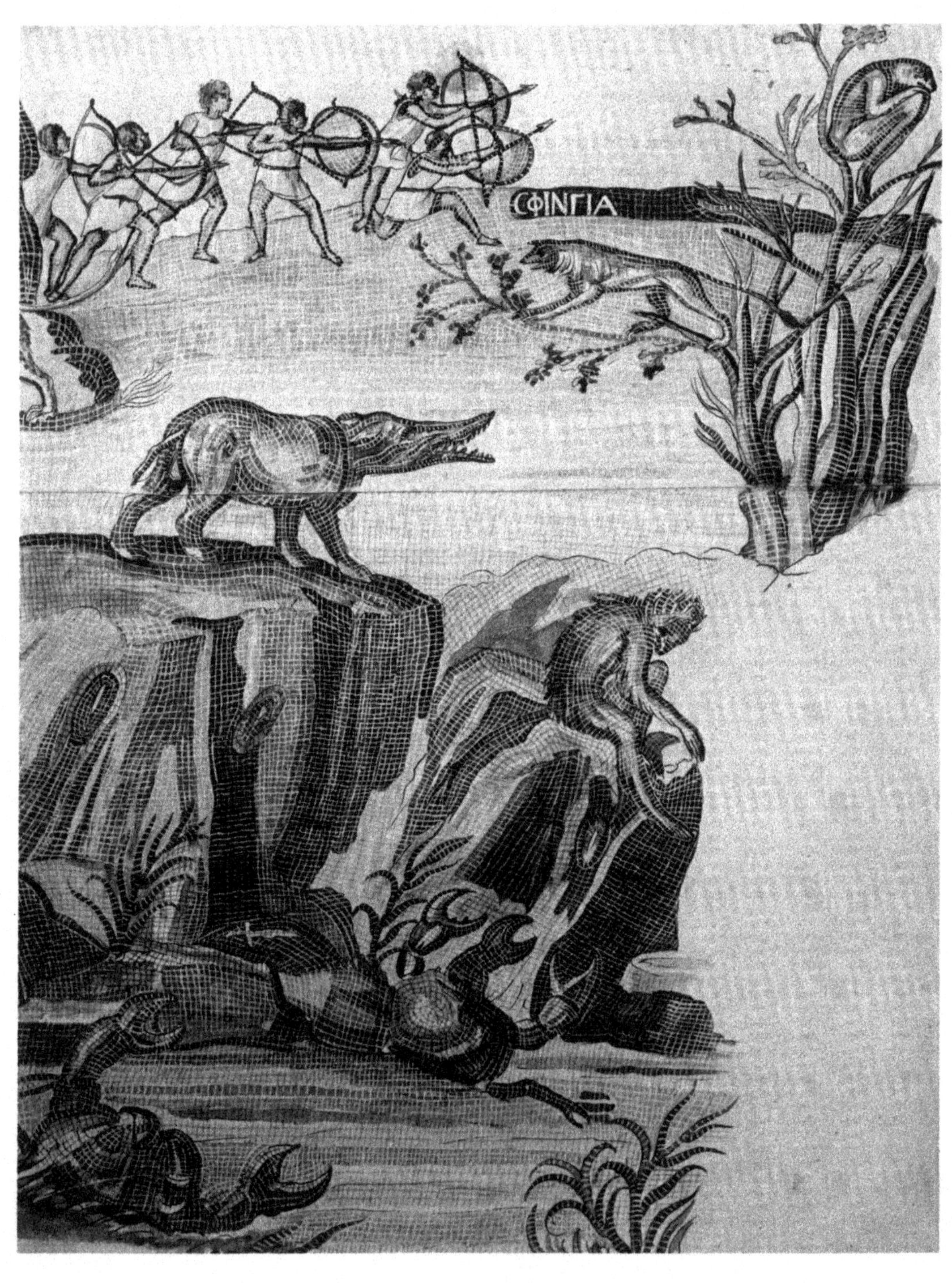

2a. Windsor drawing 19202

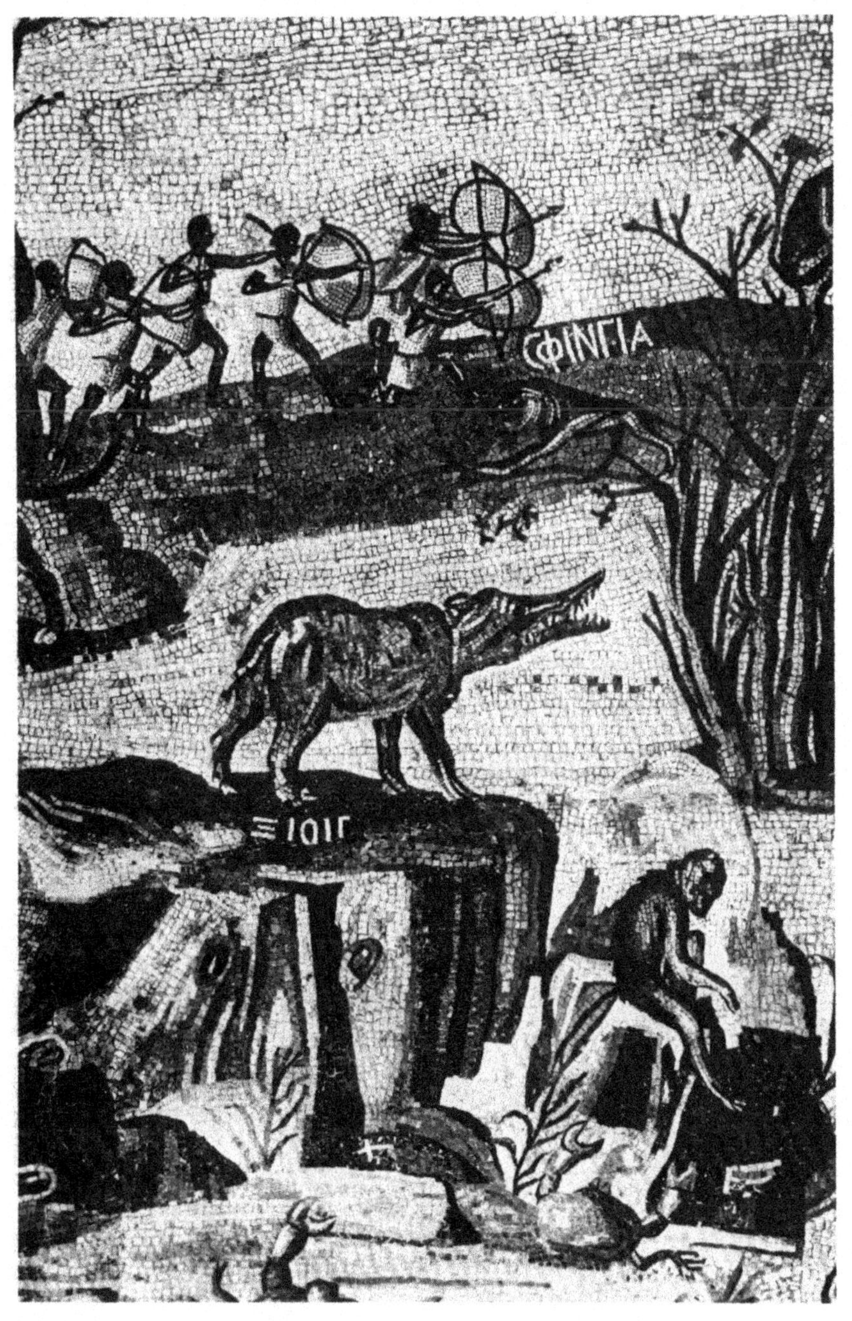

2b. The mosaic, section 2

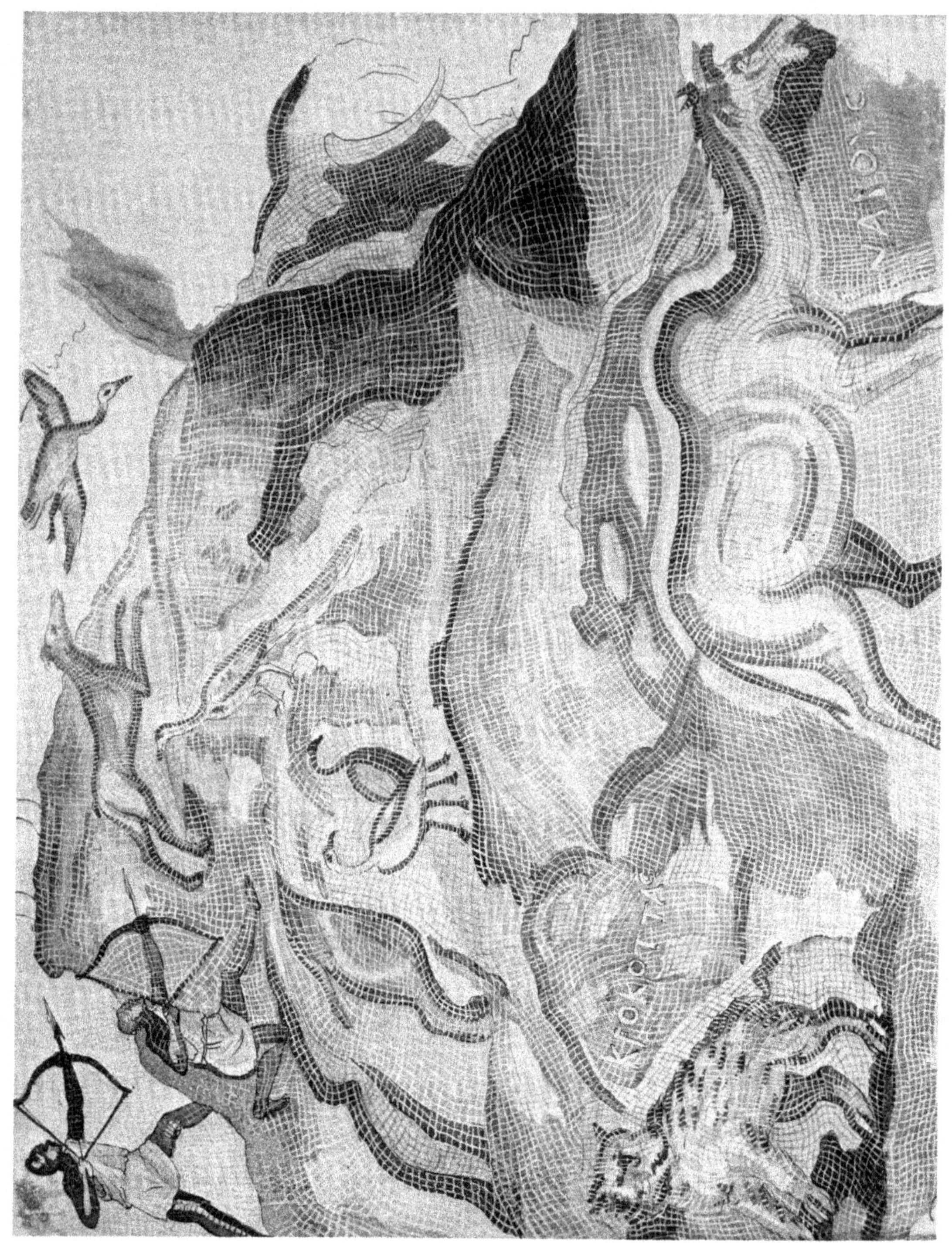

3a. Windsor drawing 19203

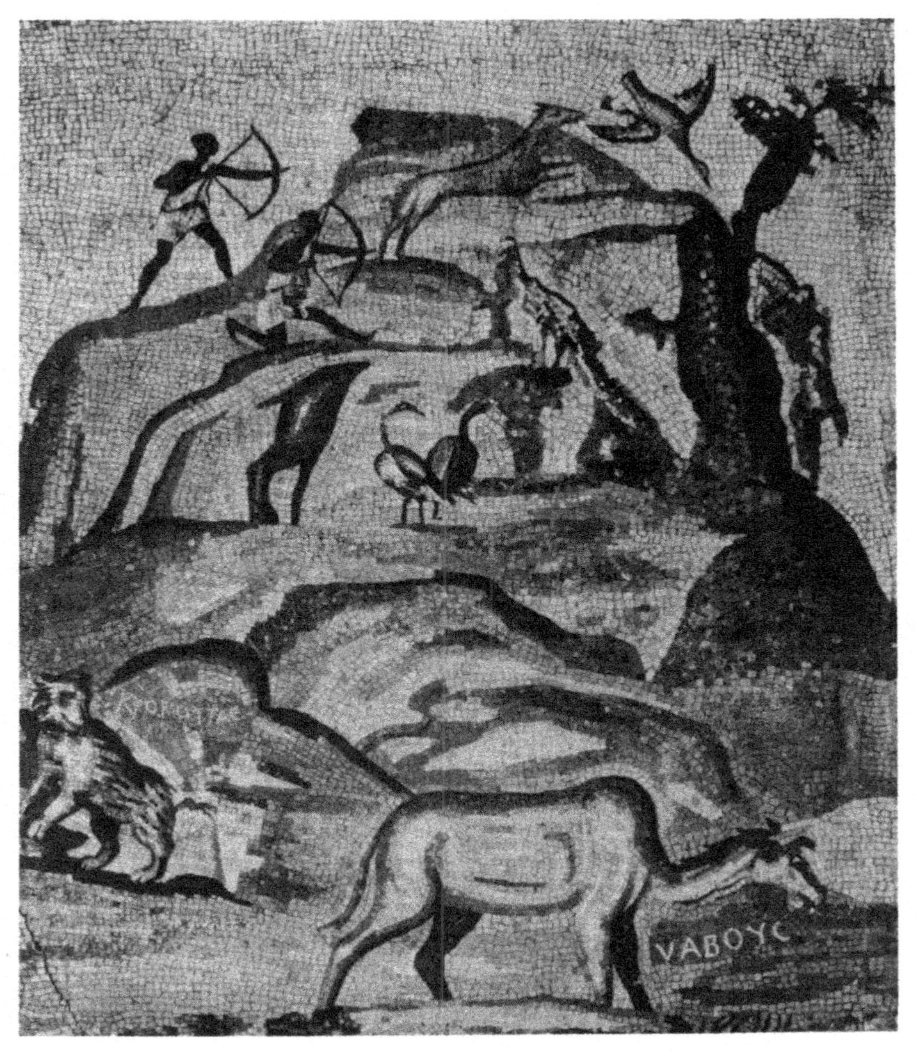

3b.

The mosaic, section 3

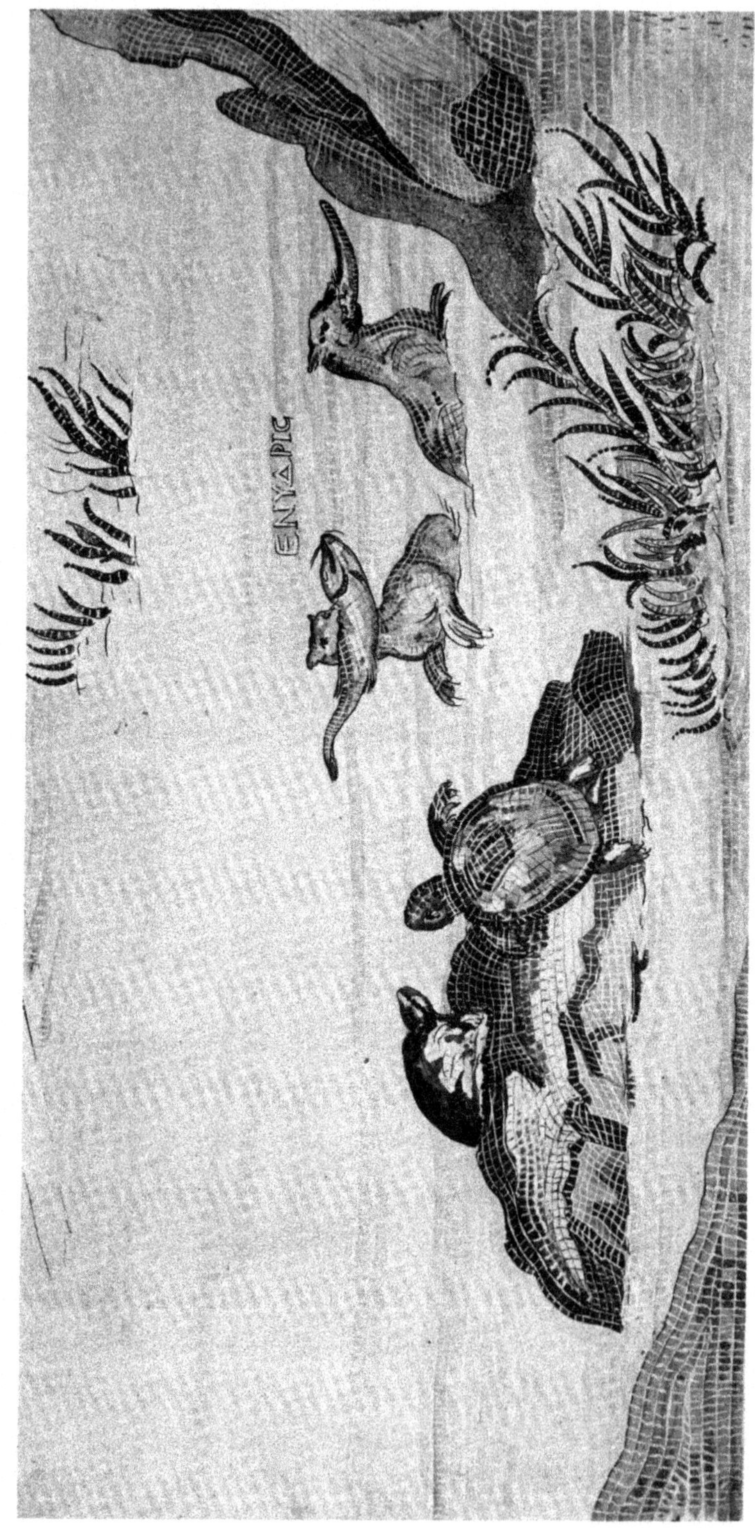

4a. Windsor drawing 19204

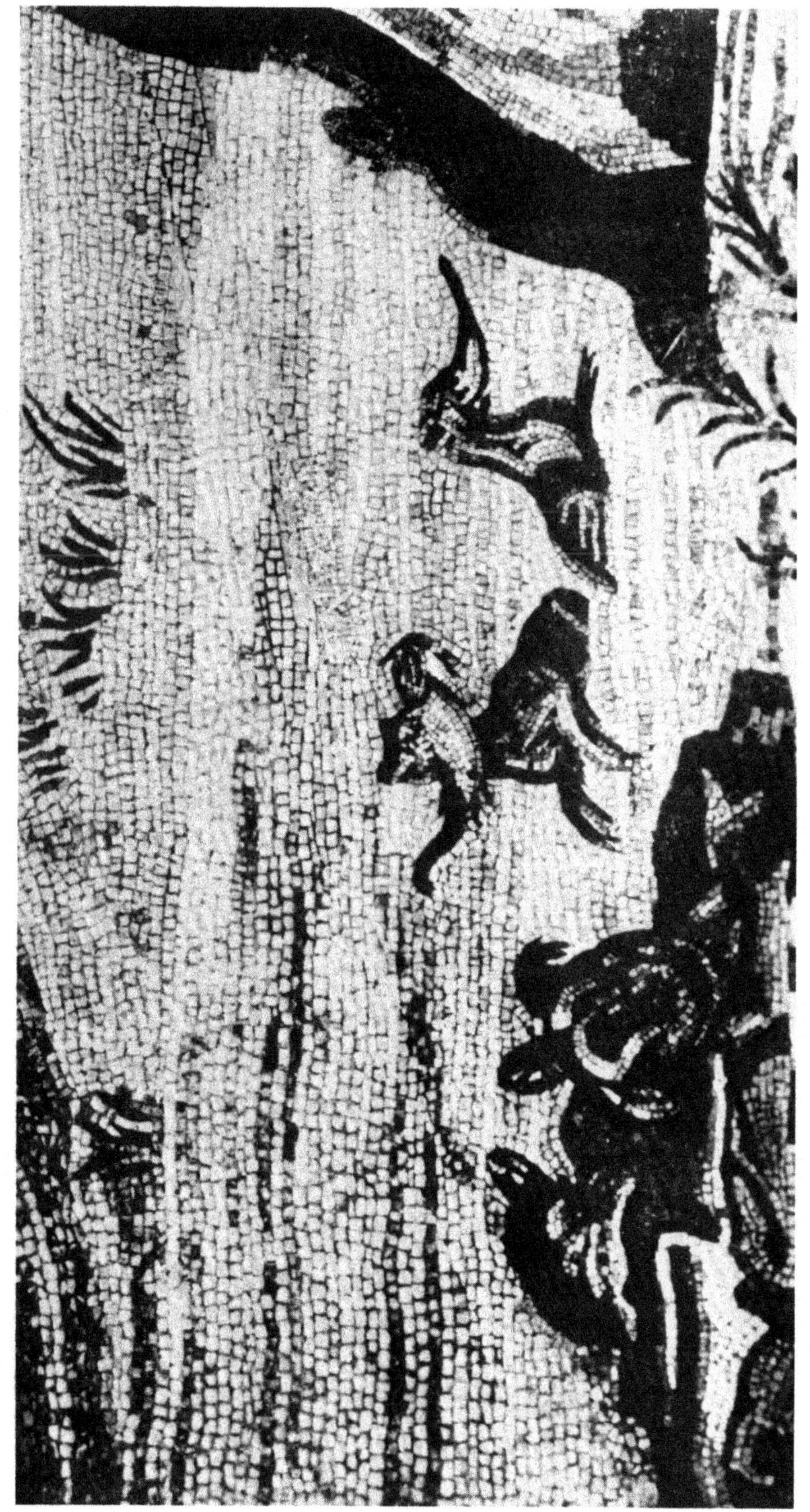

4b. The mosaic, section 4

5a. Windsor drawing 19205

5b. The mosaic, section 5

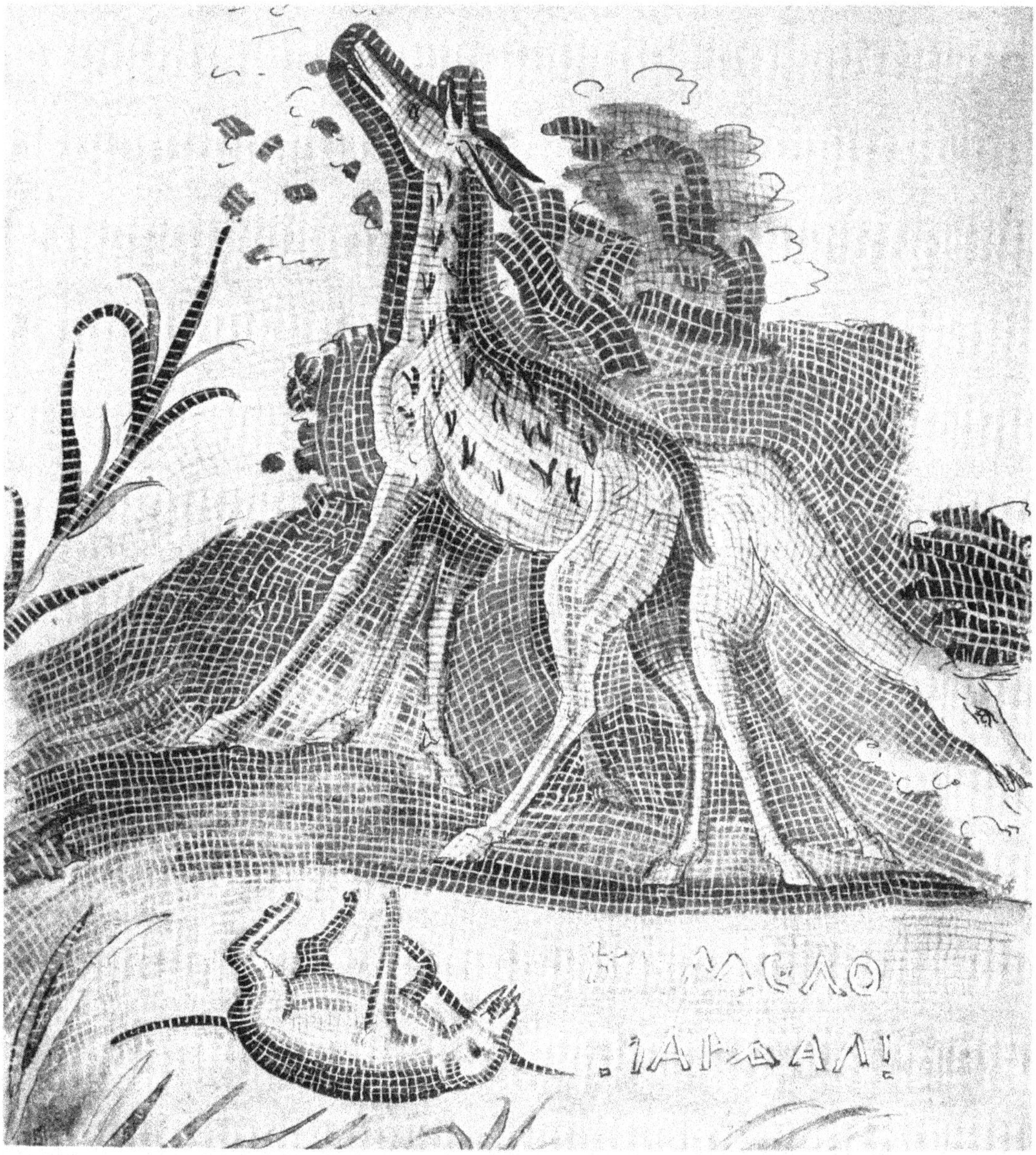

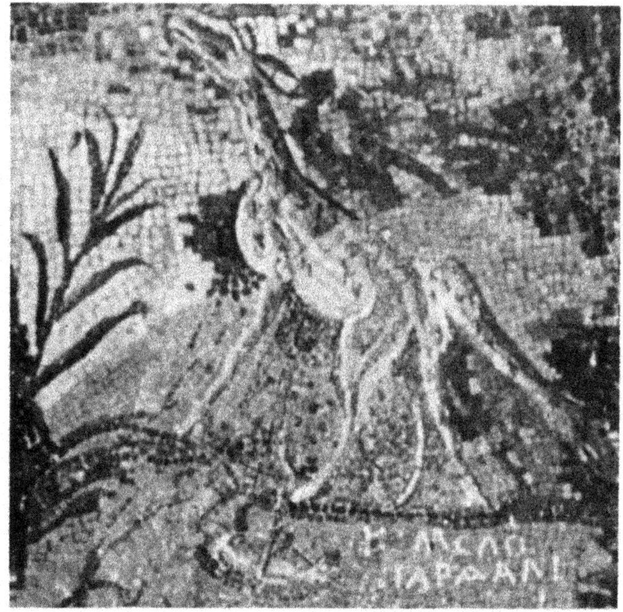

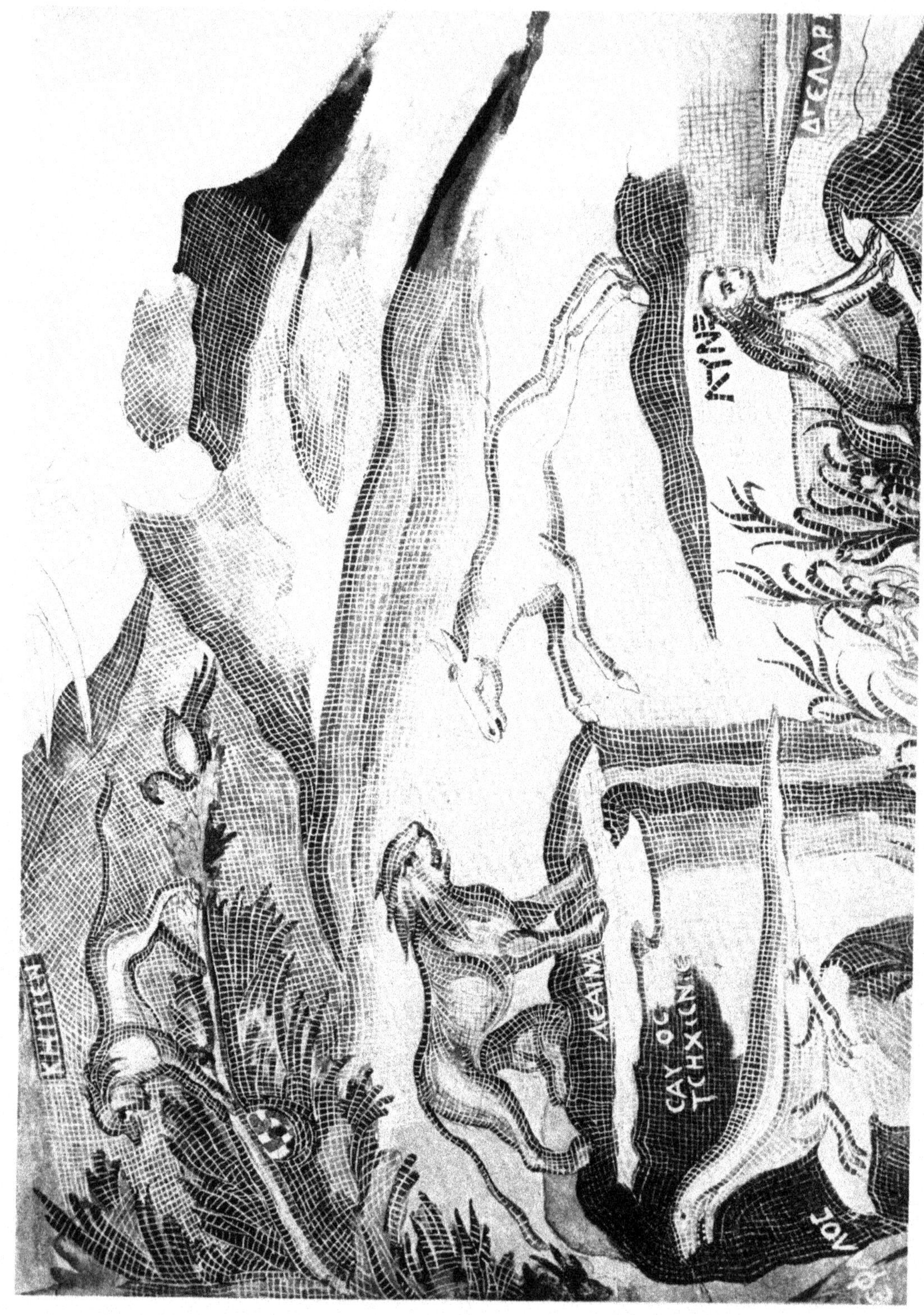

6a. Windsor drawing 19206

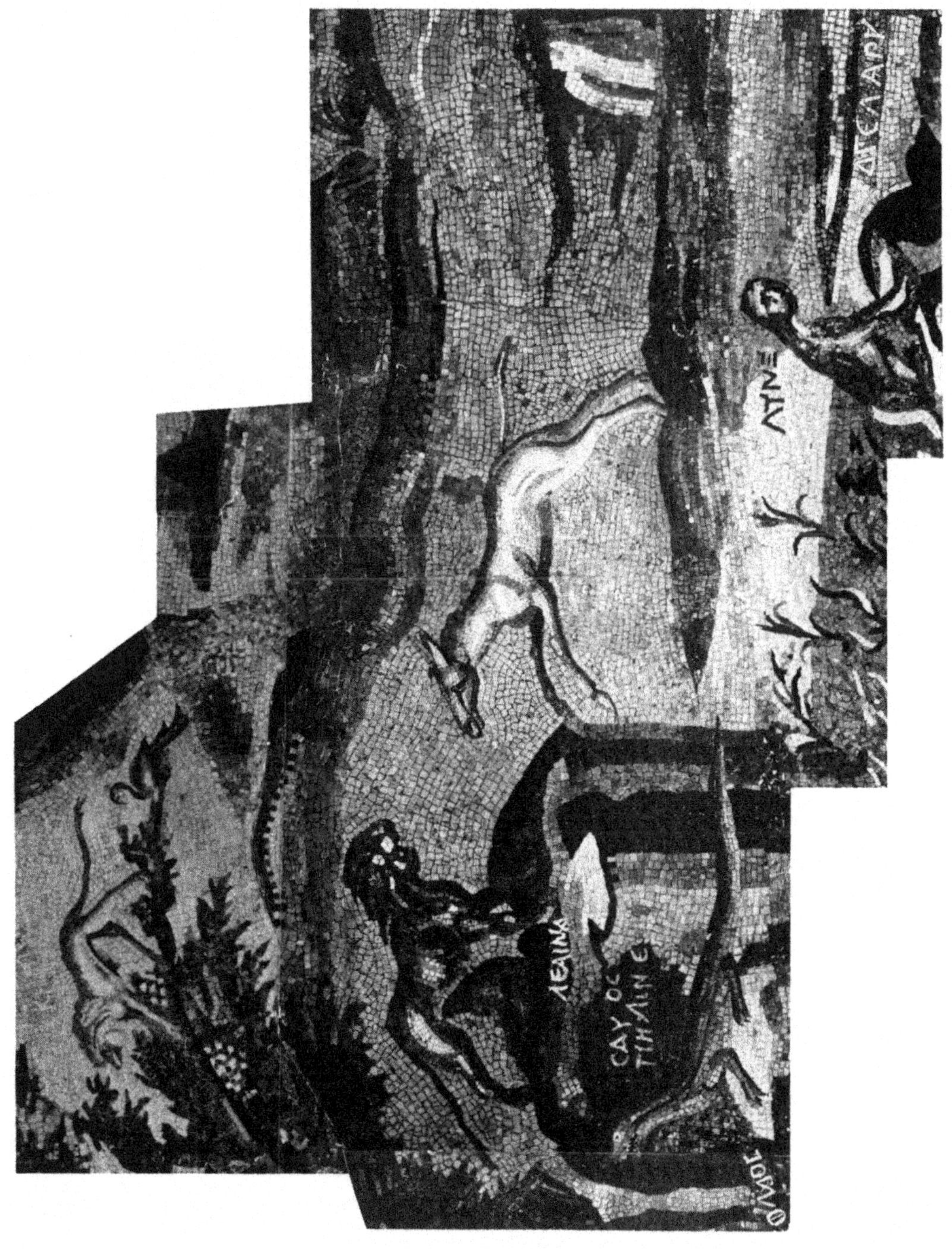

6b. The mosaic, section 6

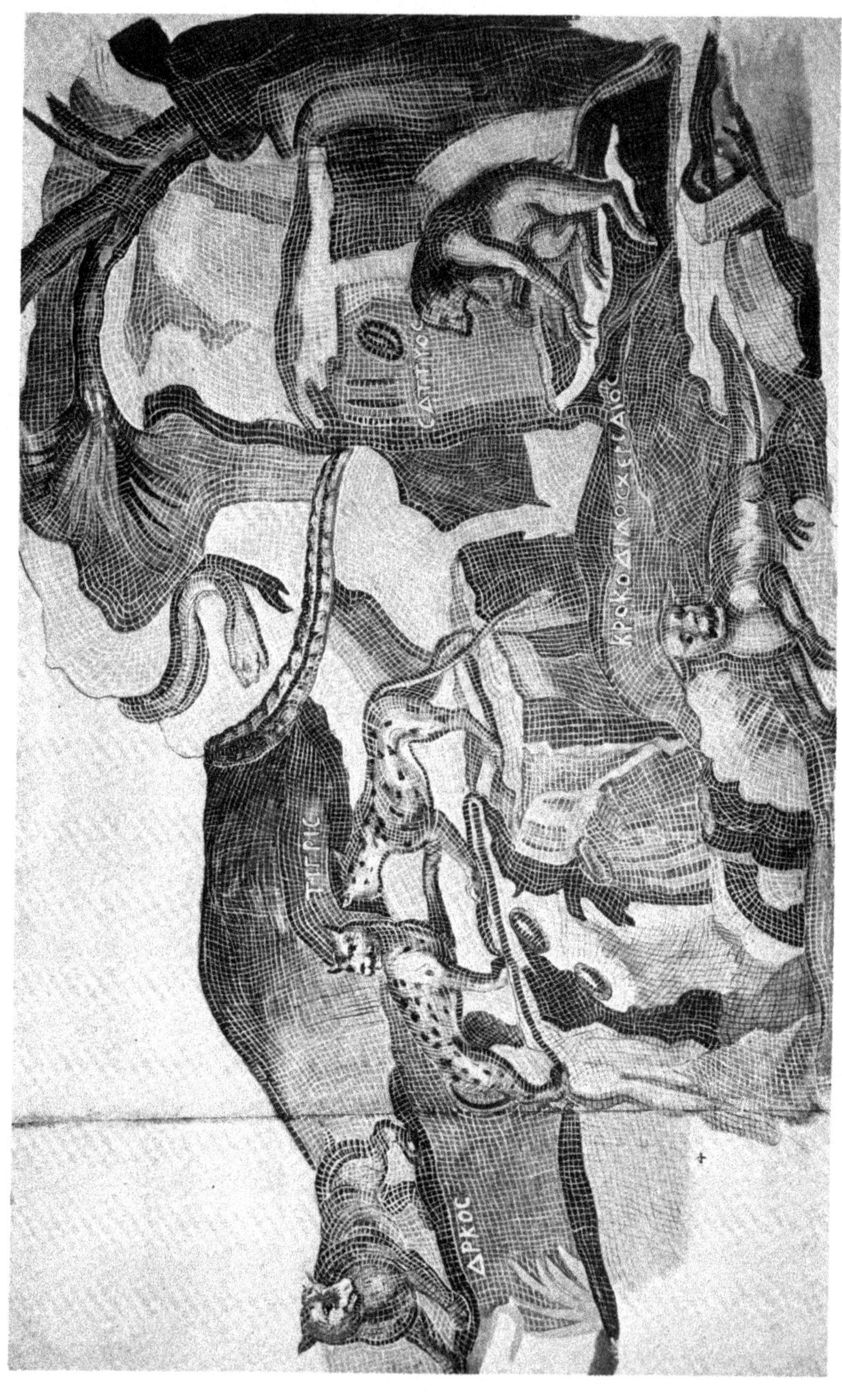

7a. Windsor drawing 19207

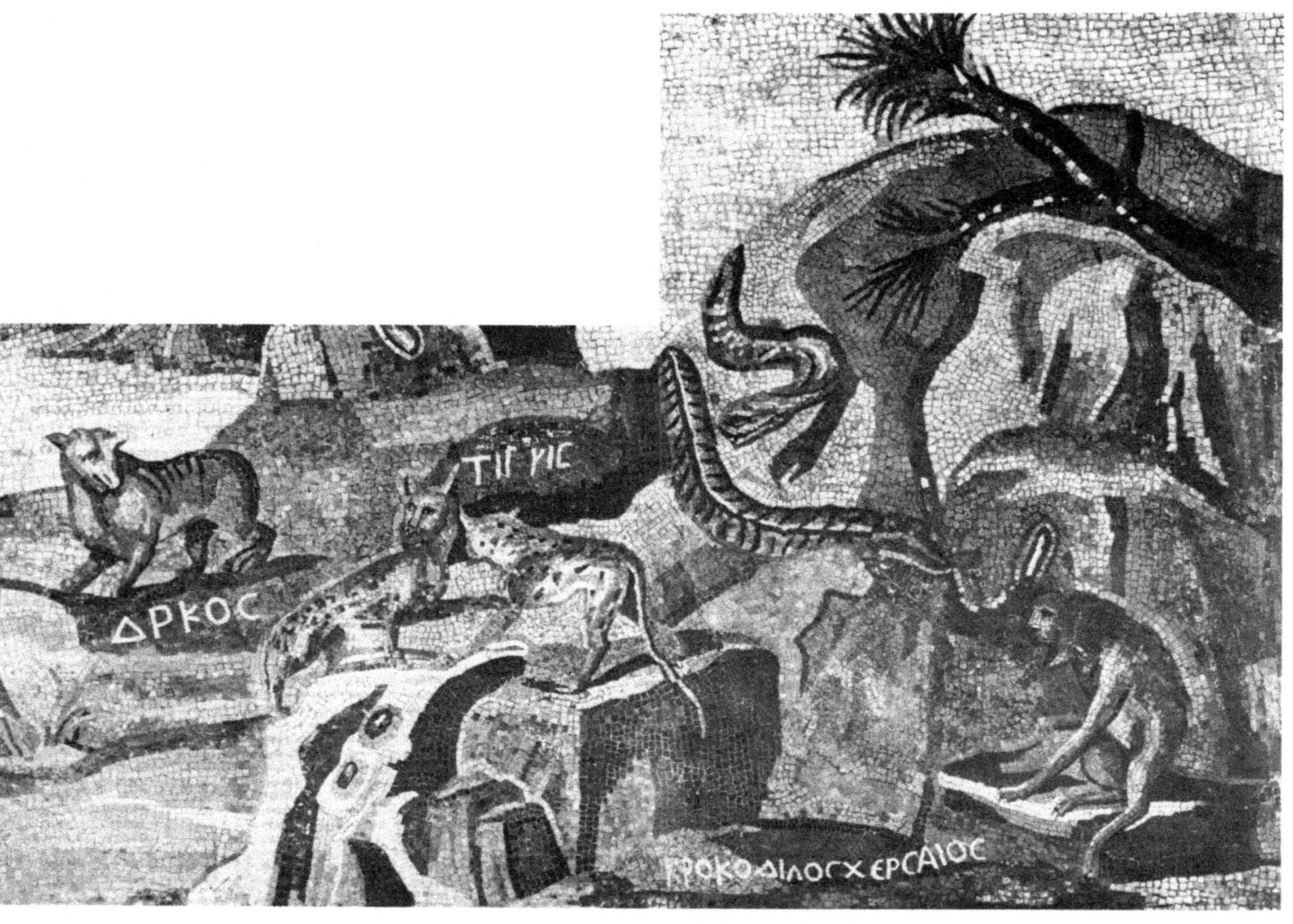

7b. The mosaic, section 7

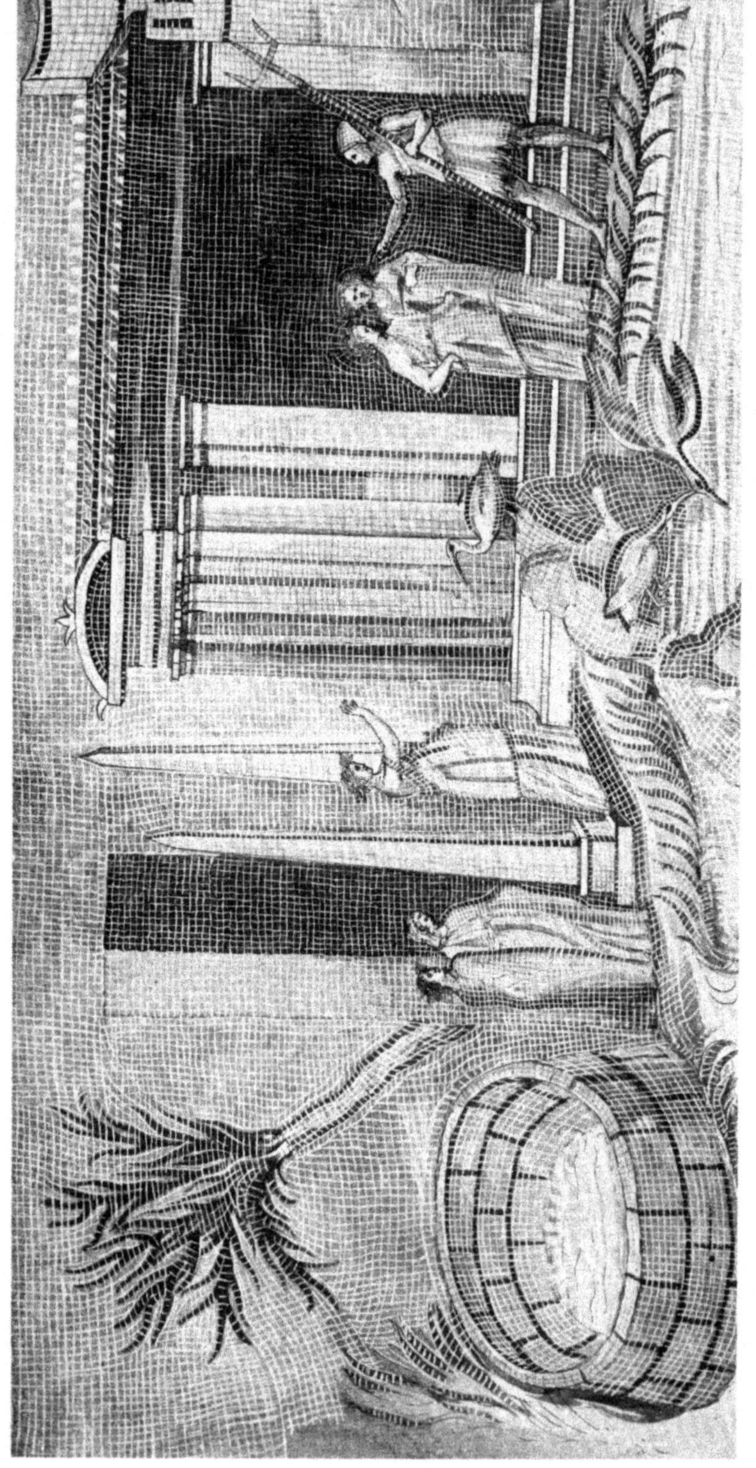

8a. Windsor drawing 19208

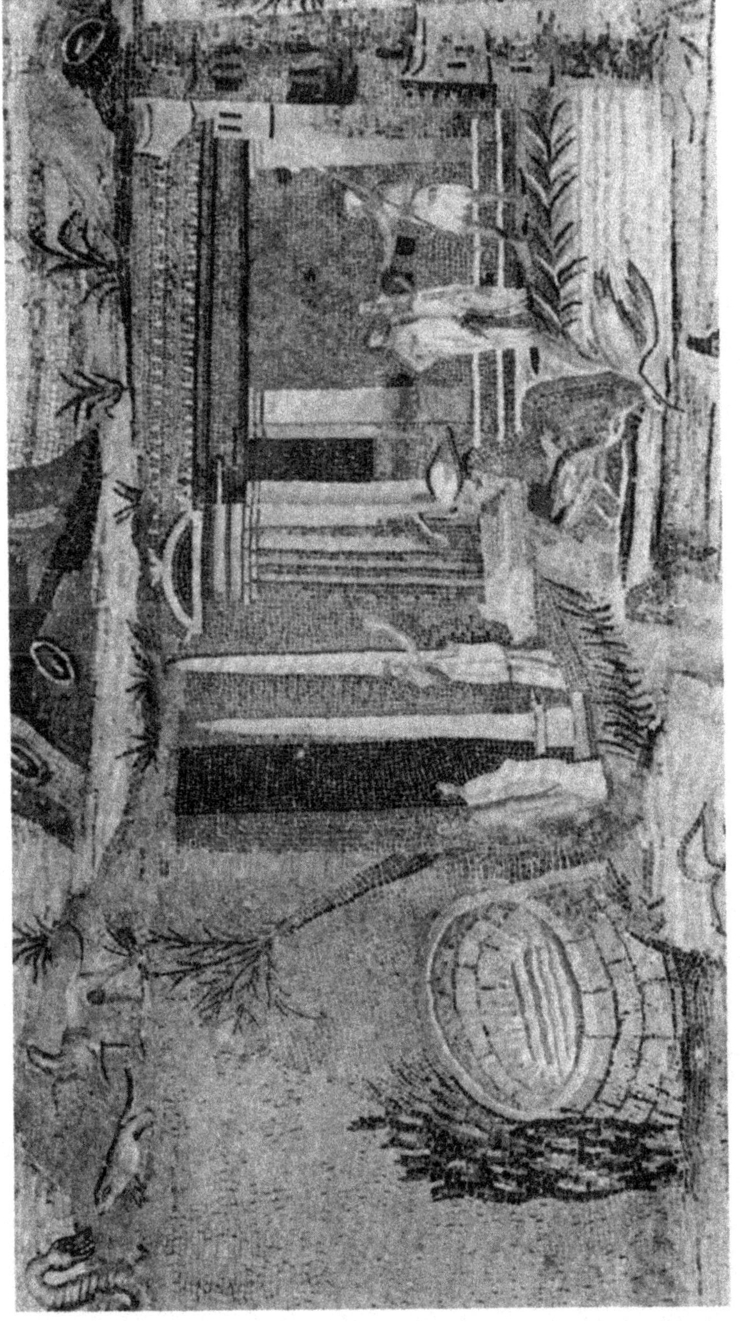

8b. The mosaic, section 8

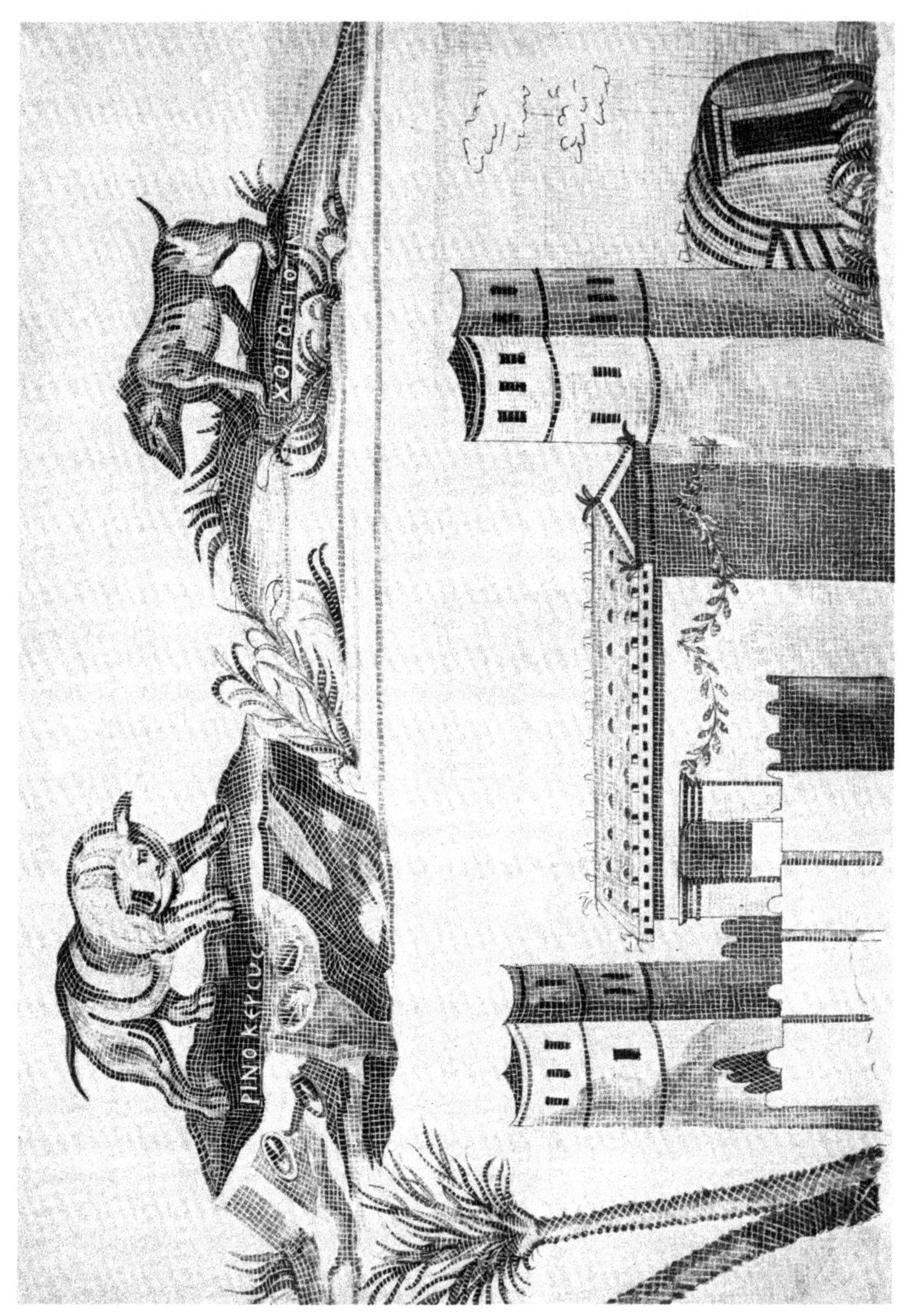

9a. Windsor drawing 19209

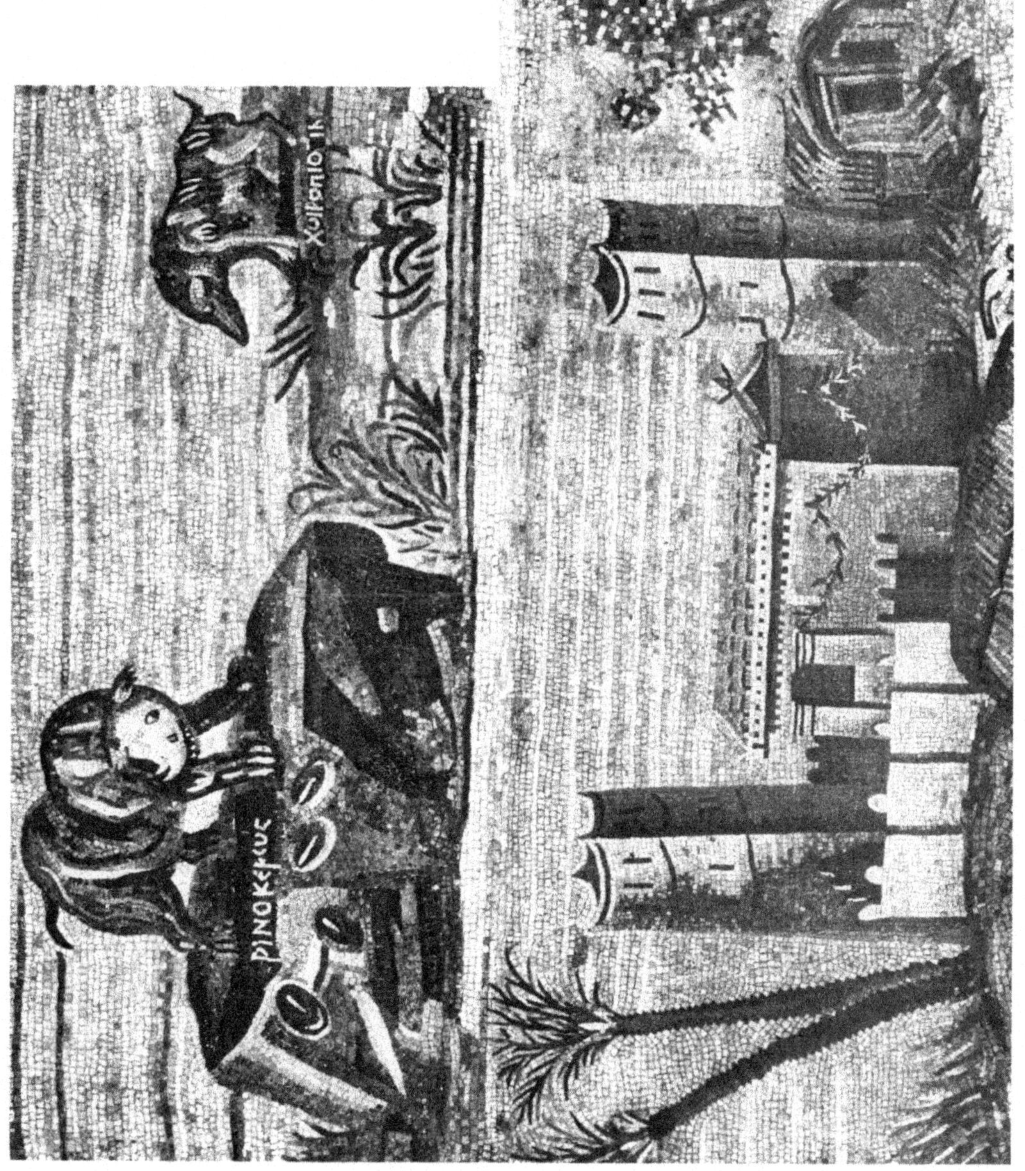

9b. The mosaic, section 9

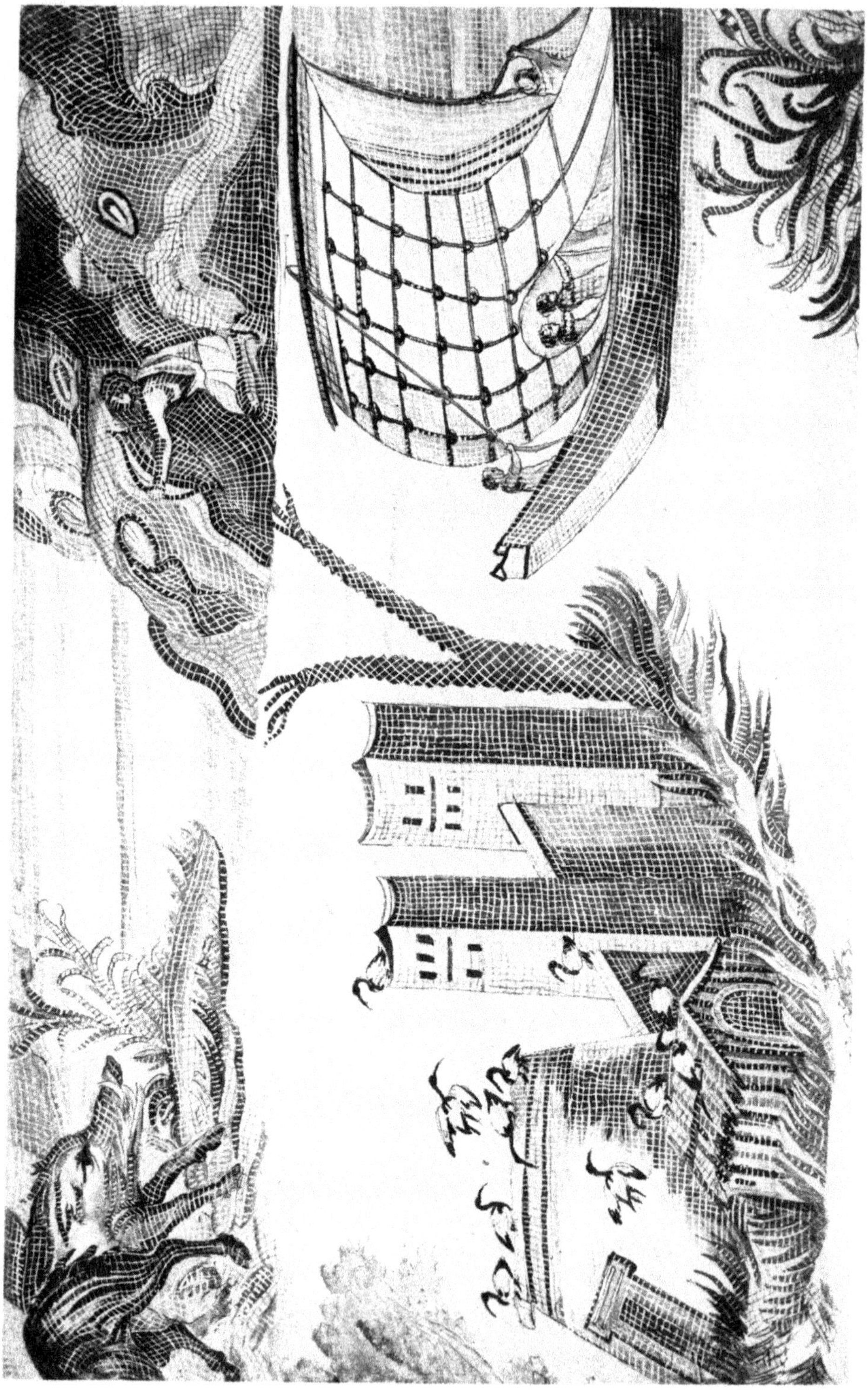

10a. Windsor drawing 19210

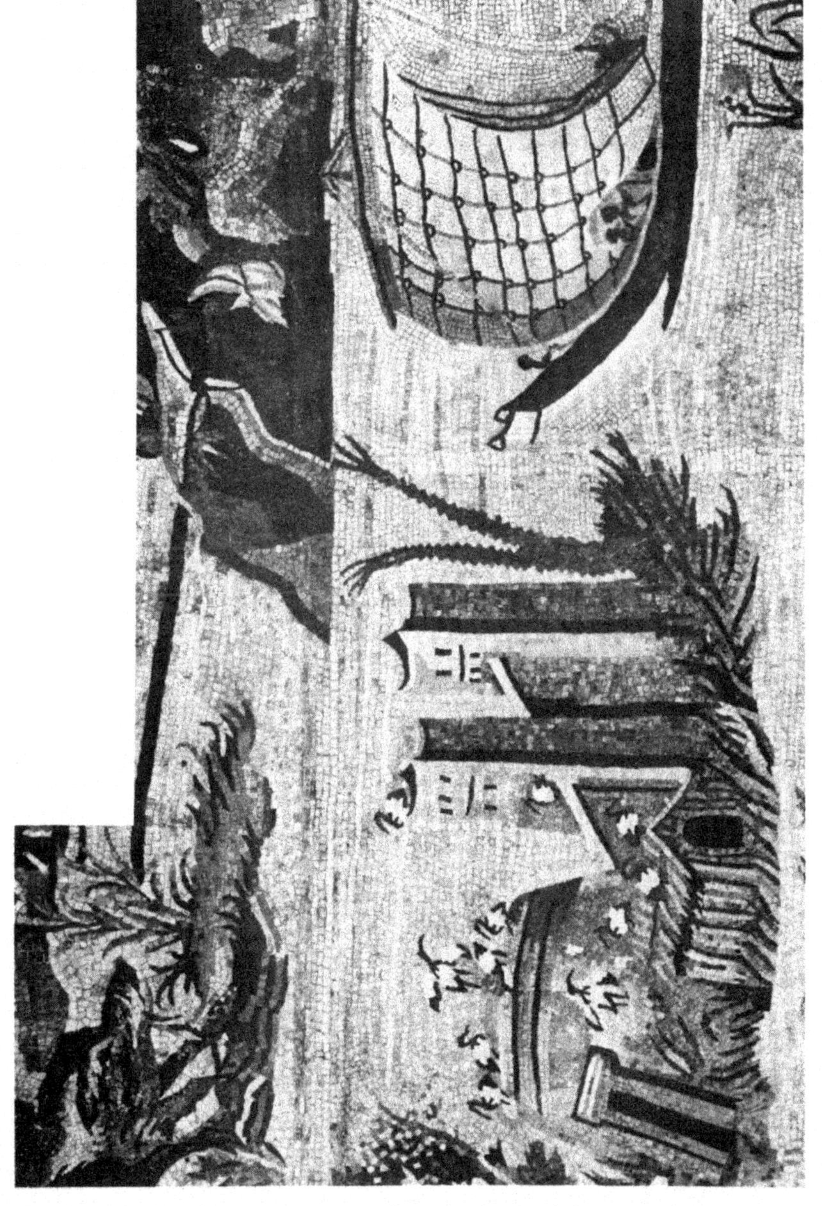

10b. The mosaic, section 10

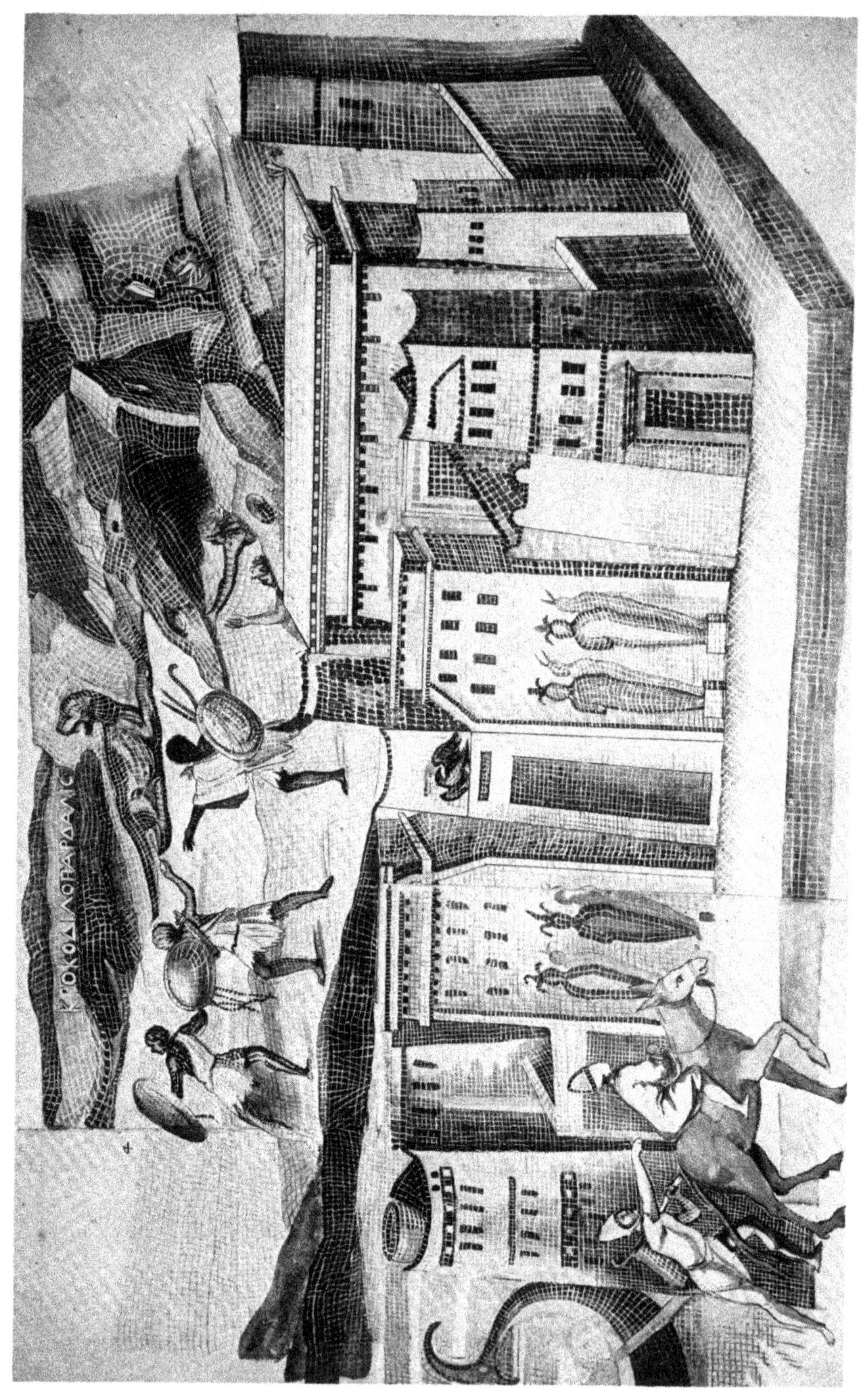

11a. Windsor drawing 19211

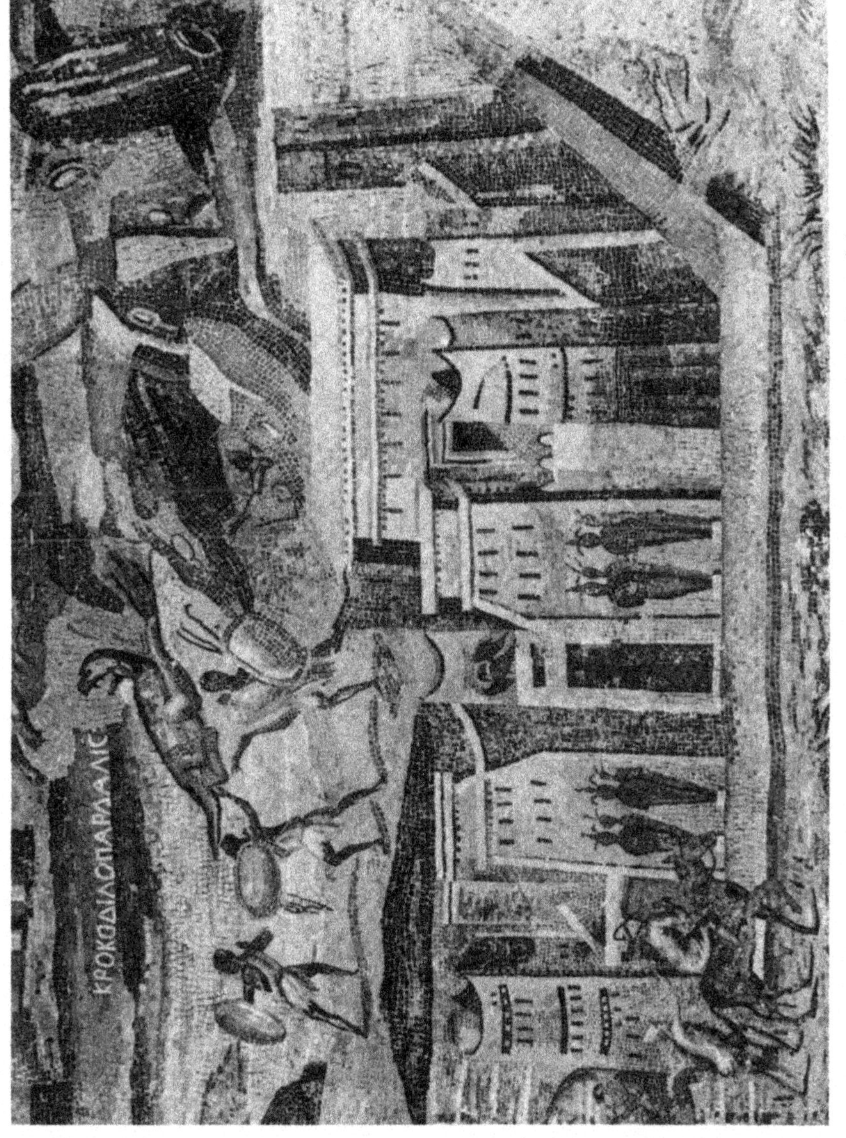

11b. The mosaic, section 11

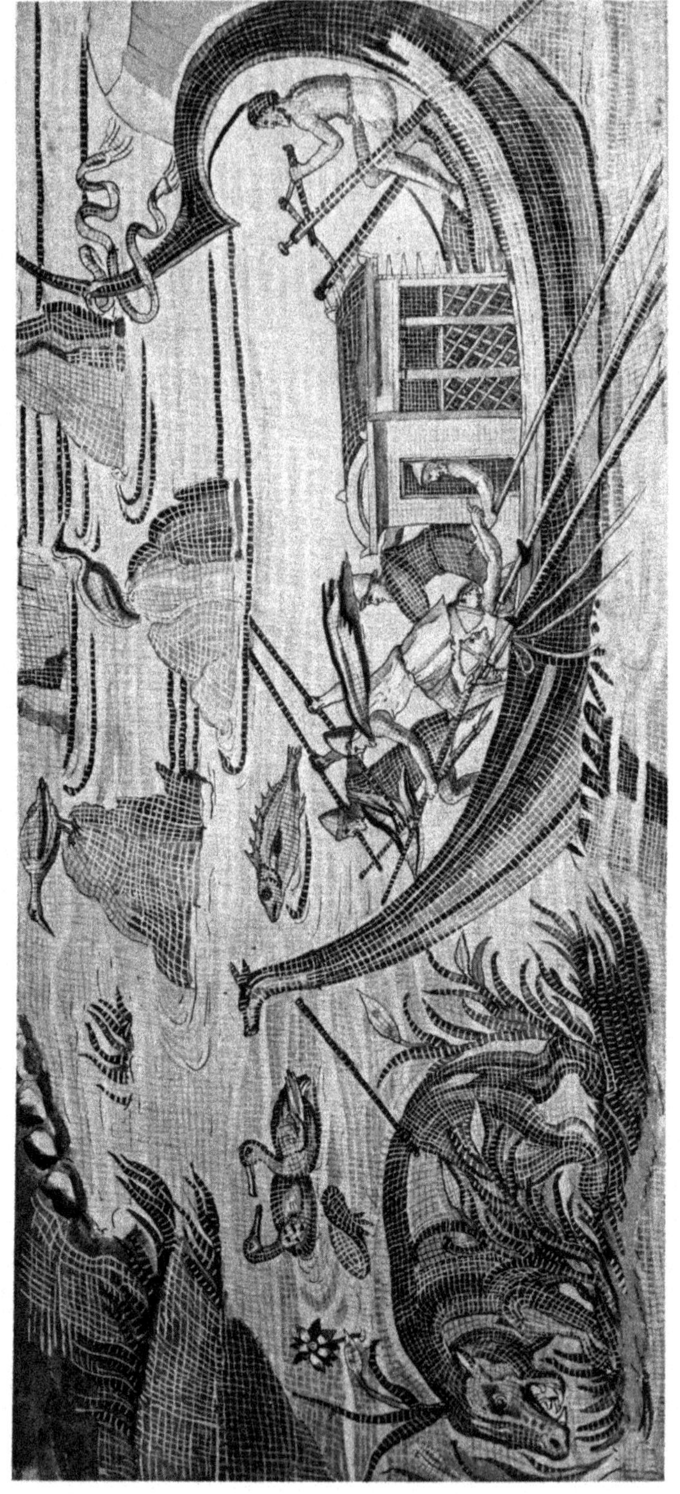

12a. Windsor drawing 19212

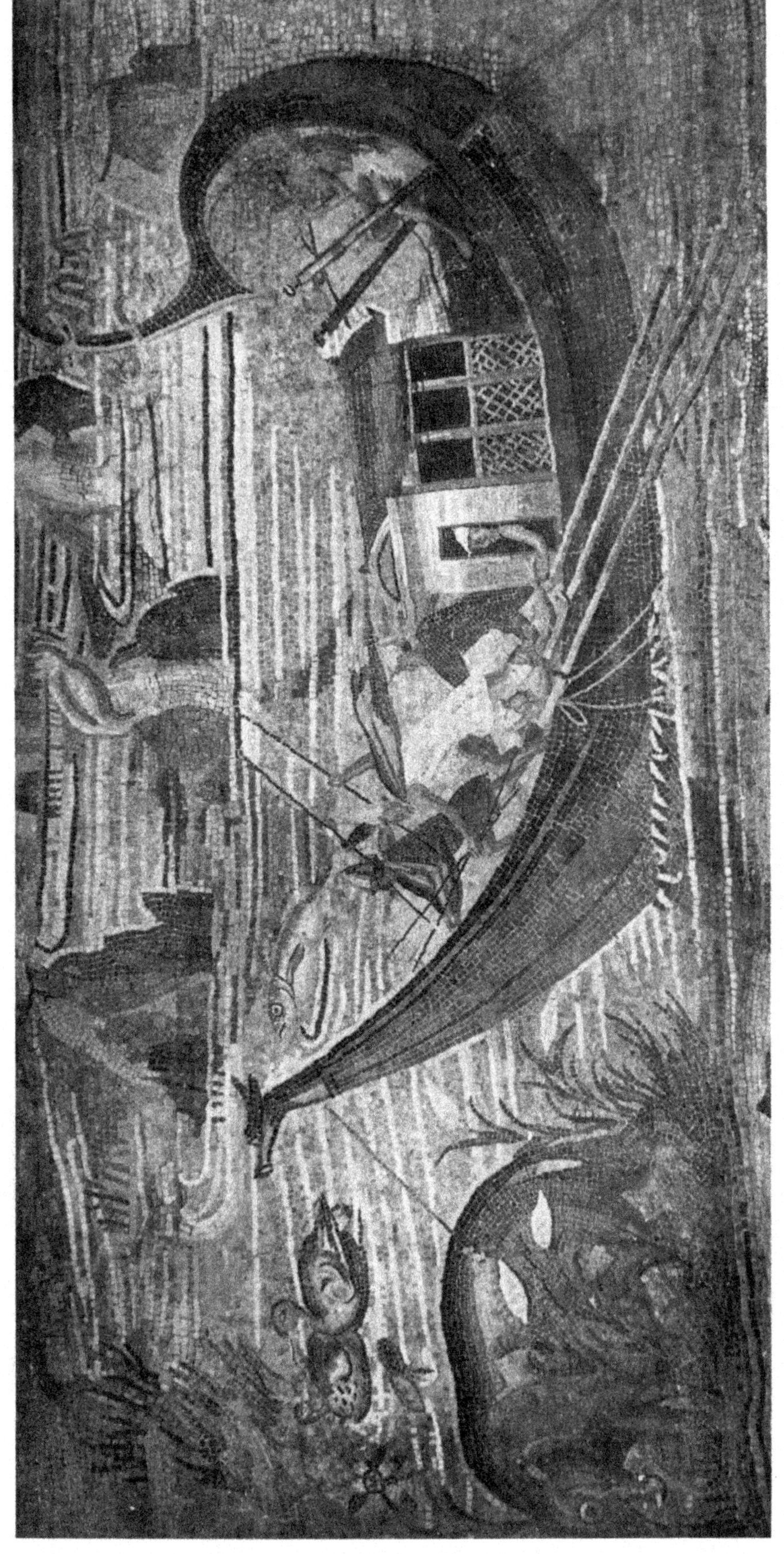

12b. The mosaic, section 12

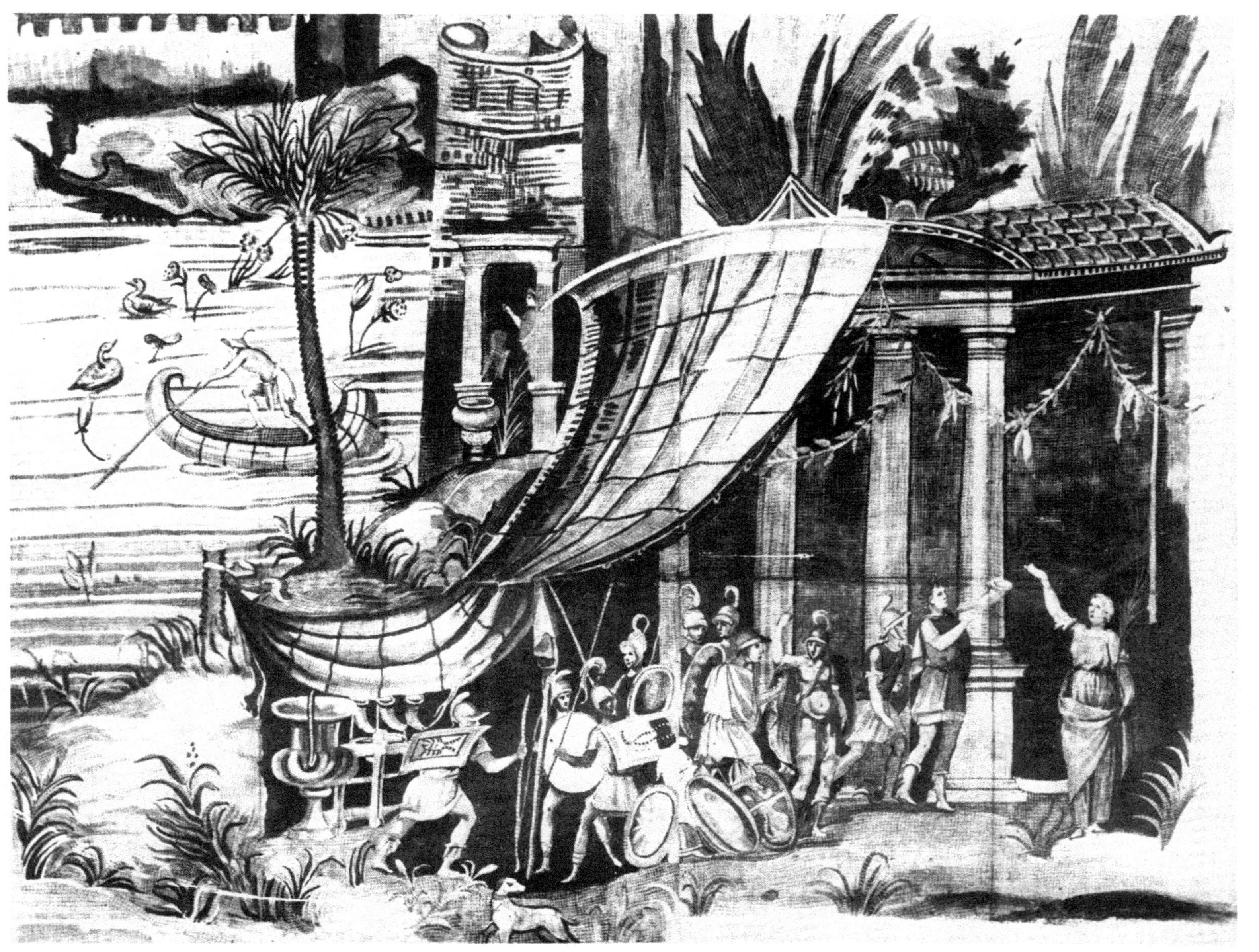

13a. Windsor drawing 19213

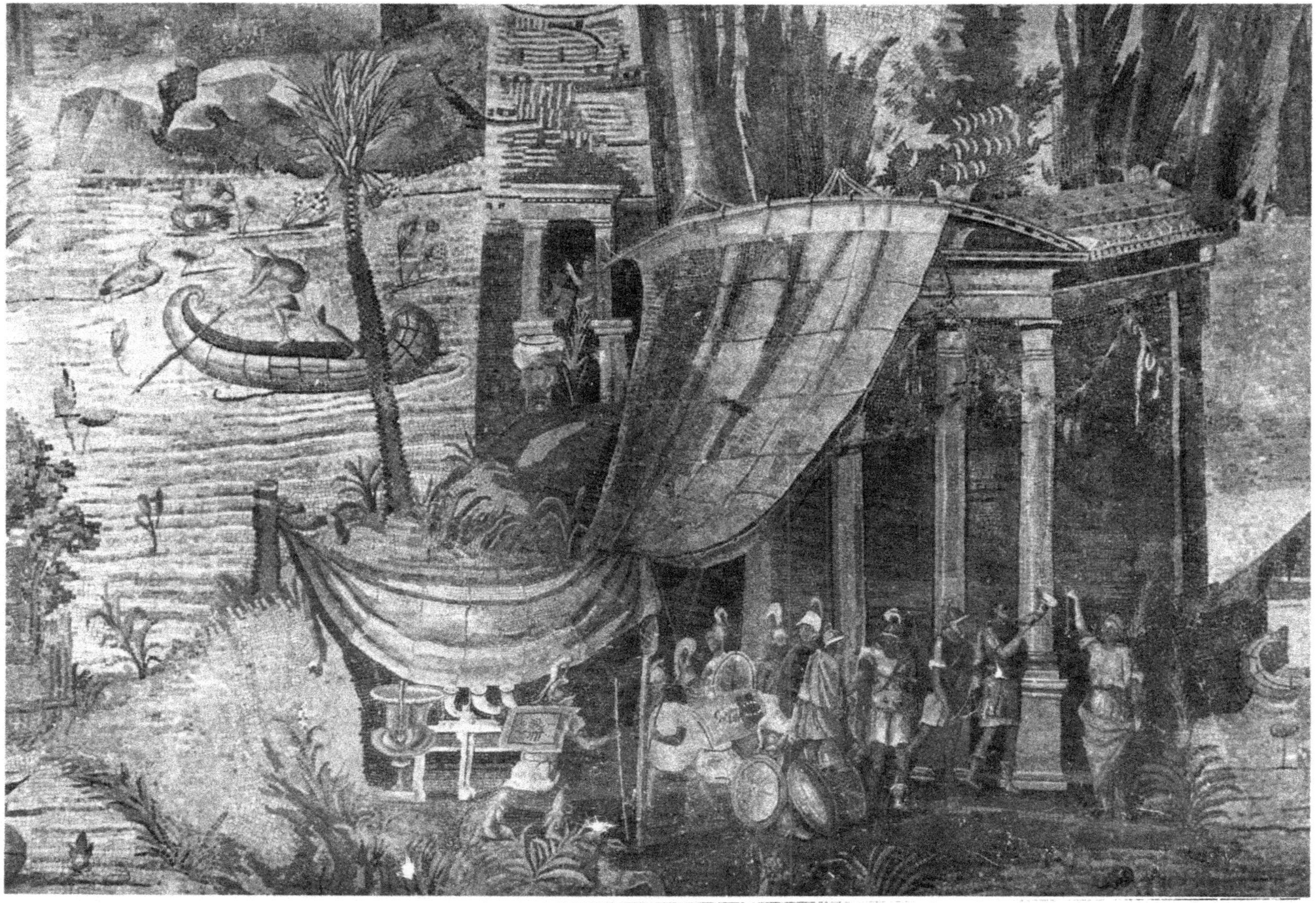

13b. The mosaic, section 13

13c. Windsor drawing 11483

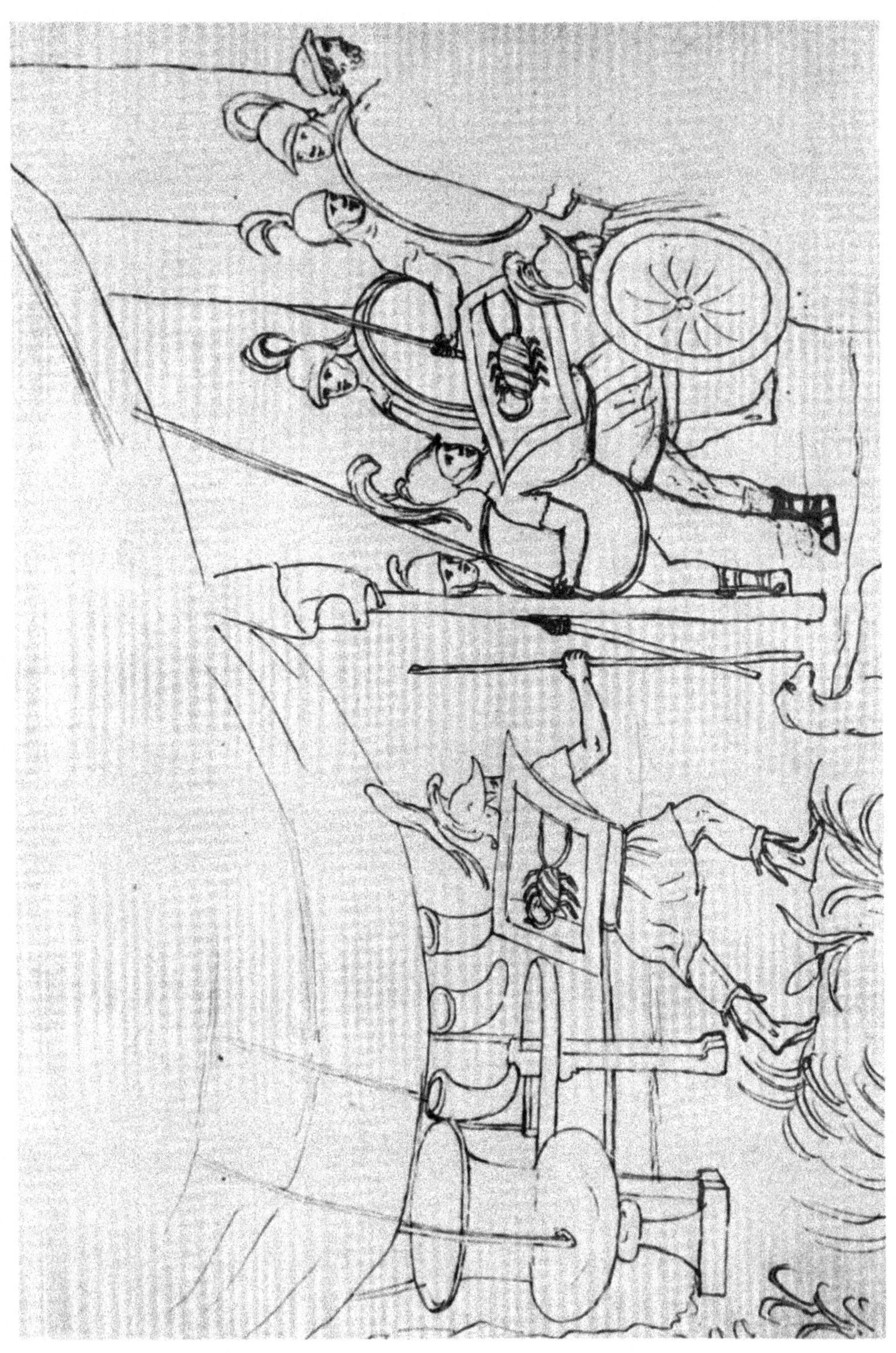

14. Windsor drawing 19214

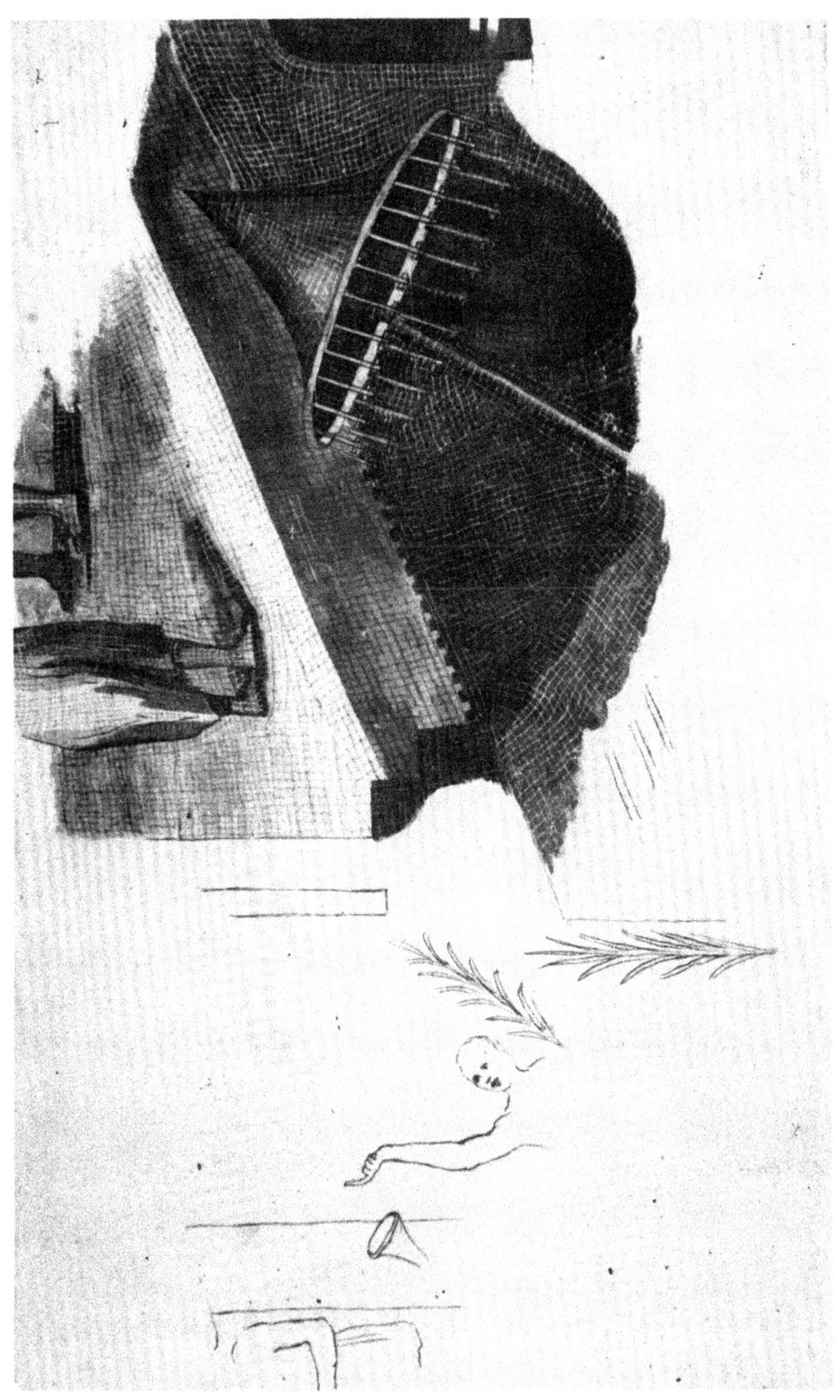

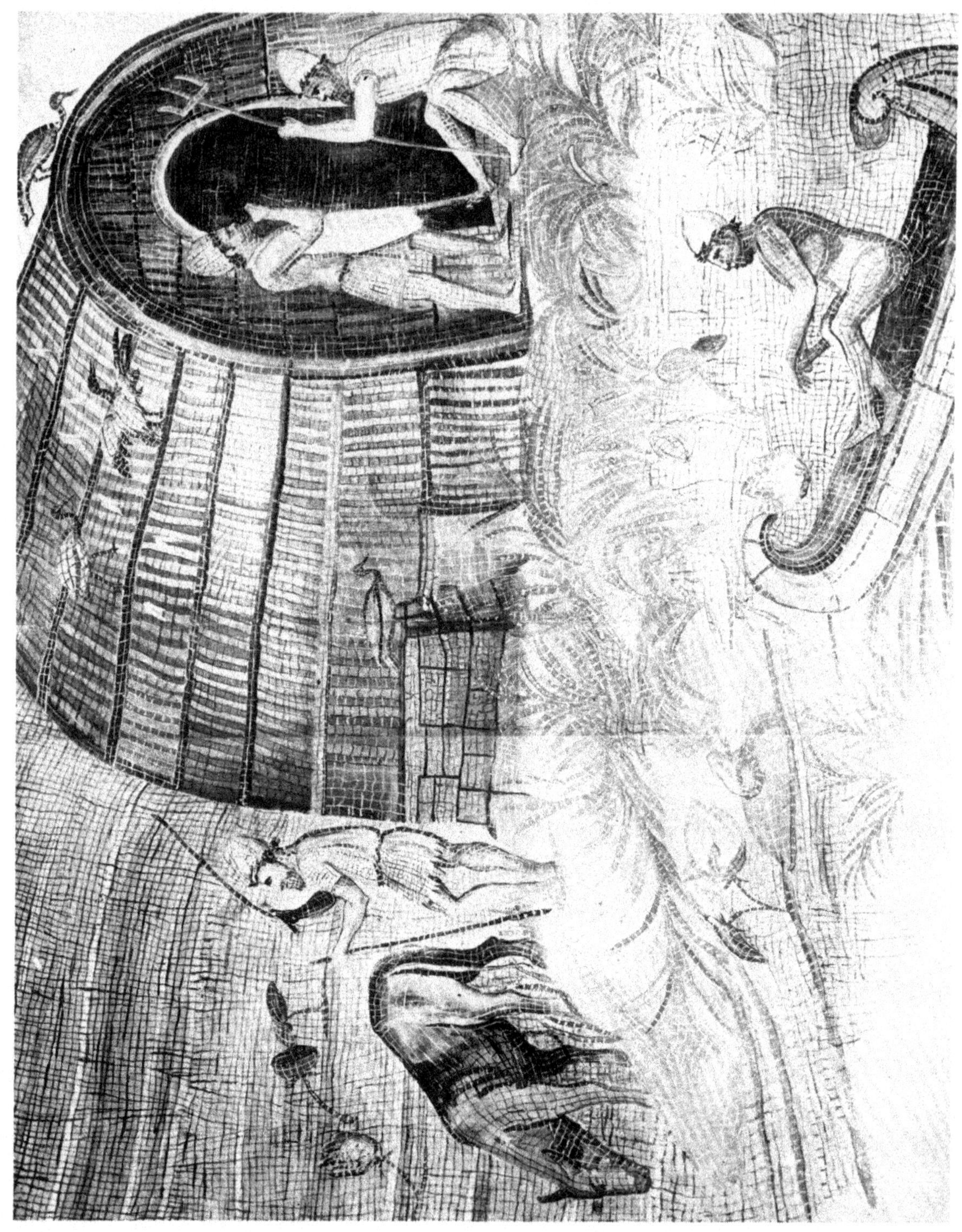

15a. Windsor drawing 19215

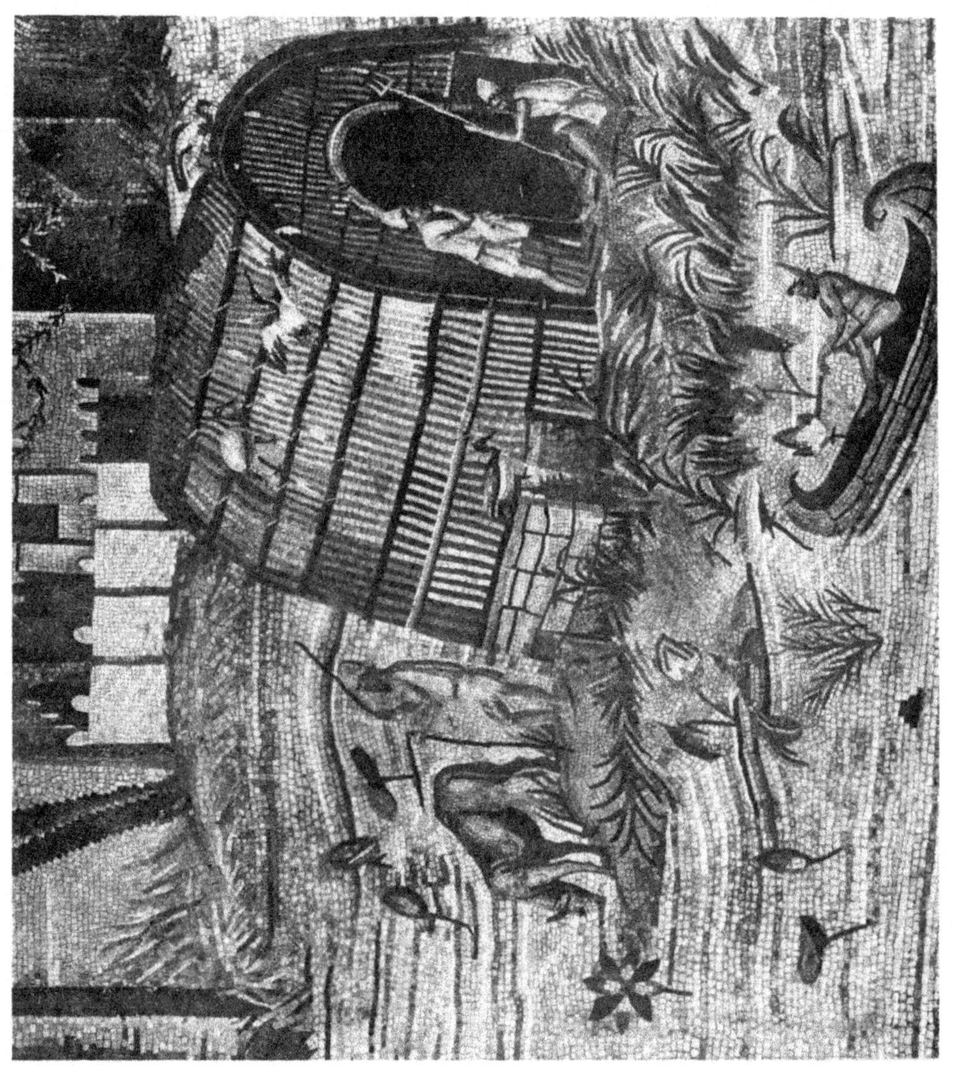

15b. The mosaic, section 15

15c. Windsor drawing 11484

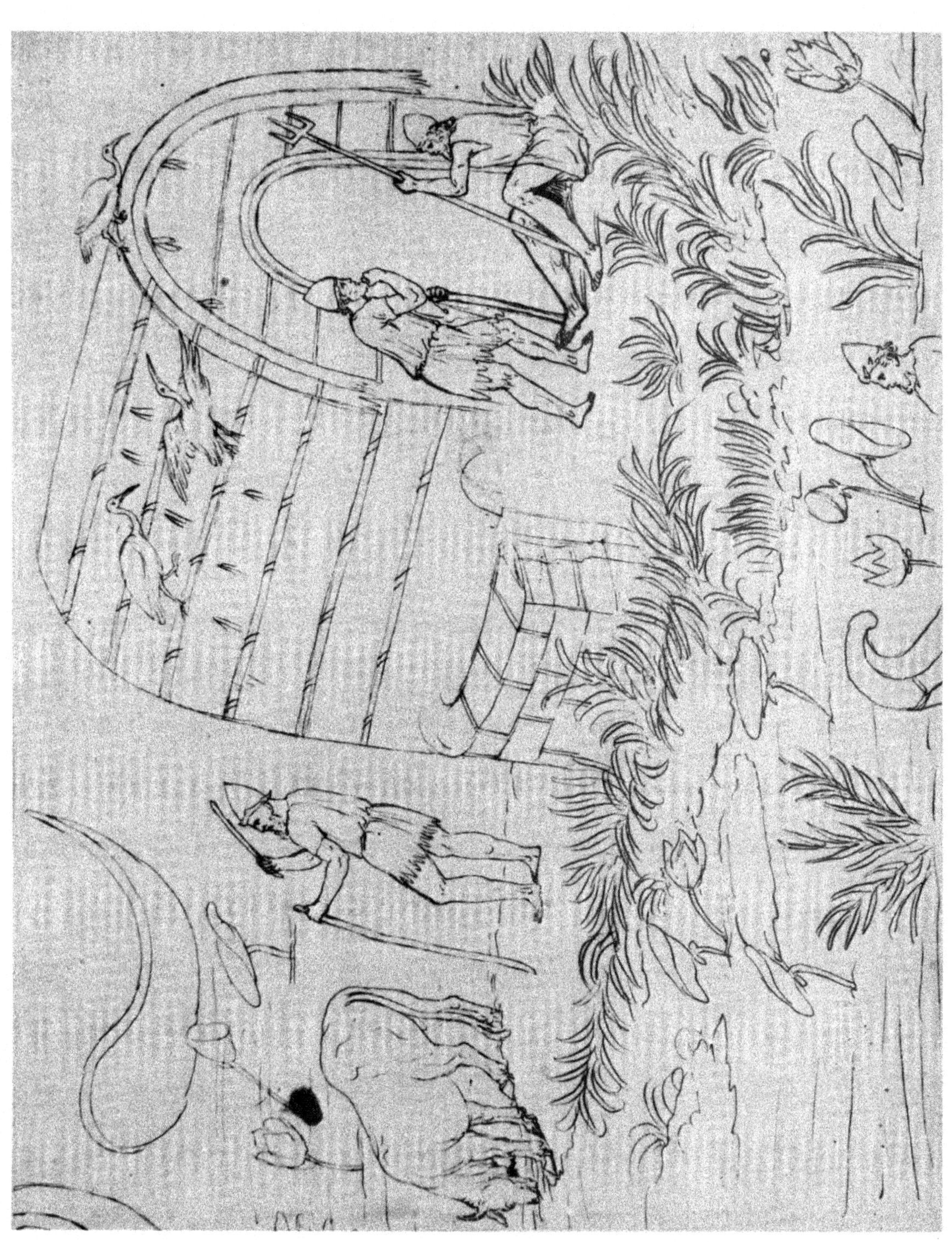

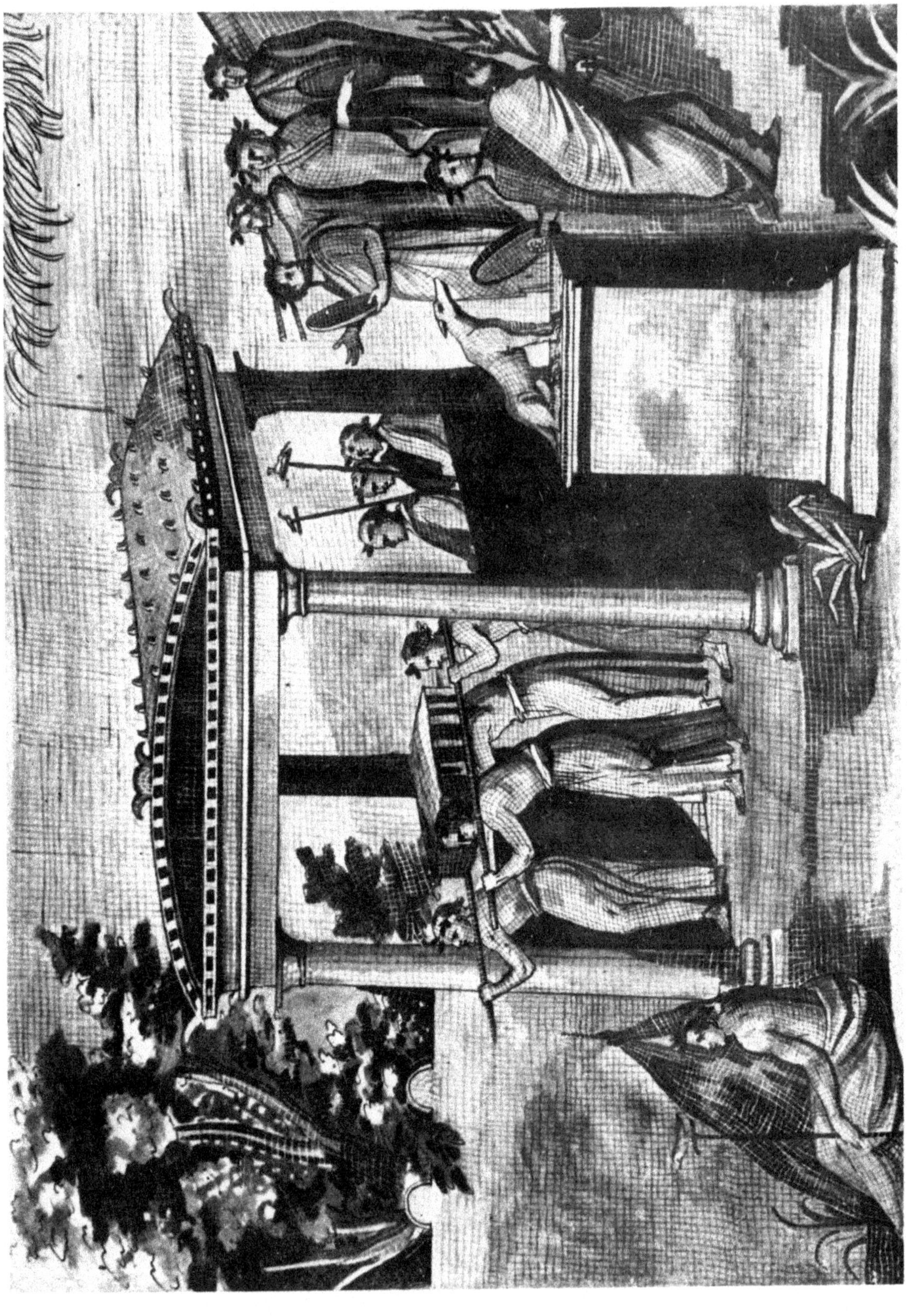

16a. Windsor drawing 19216

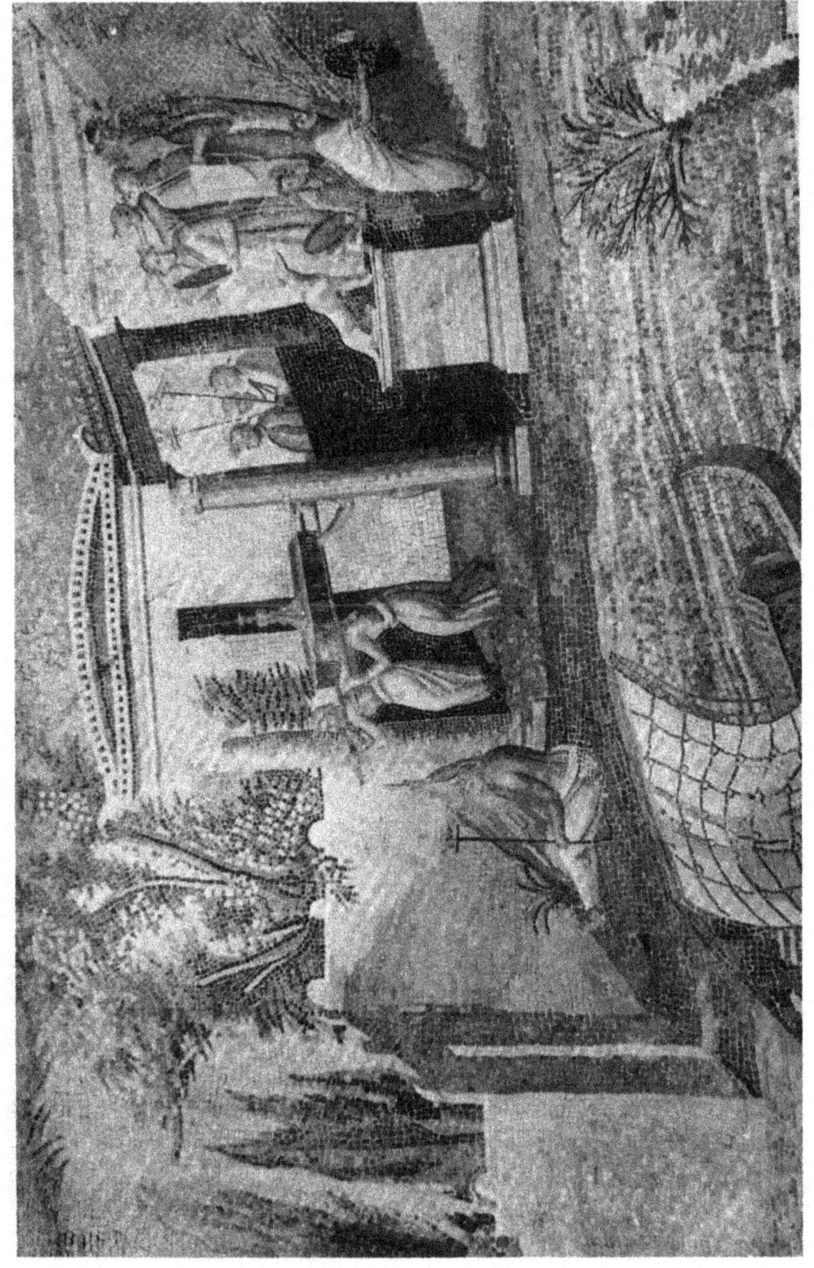

16b. The mosaic, section 16

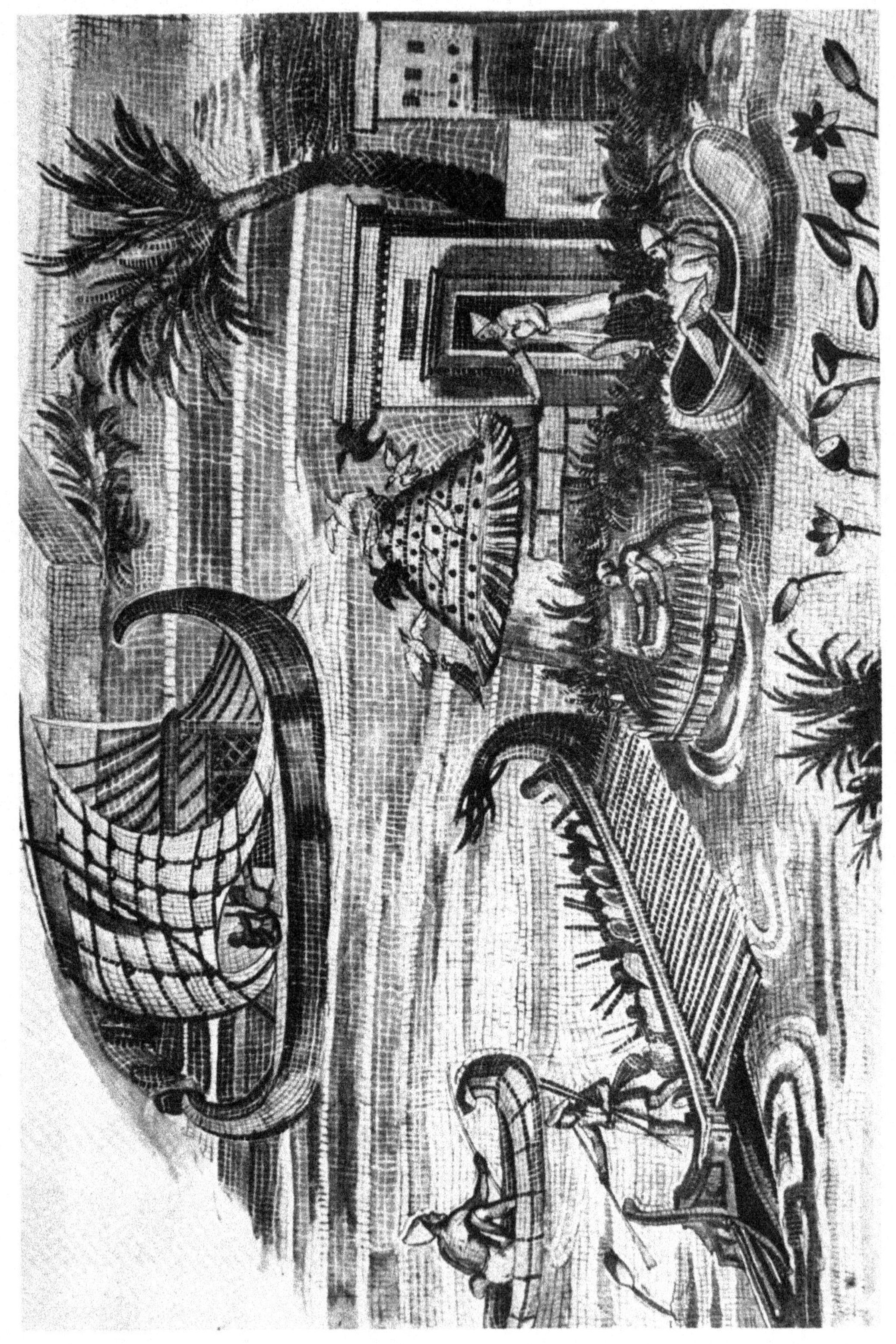

17a. Windsor drawing 19217

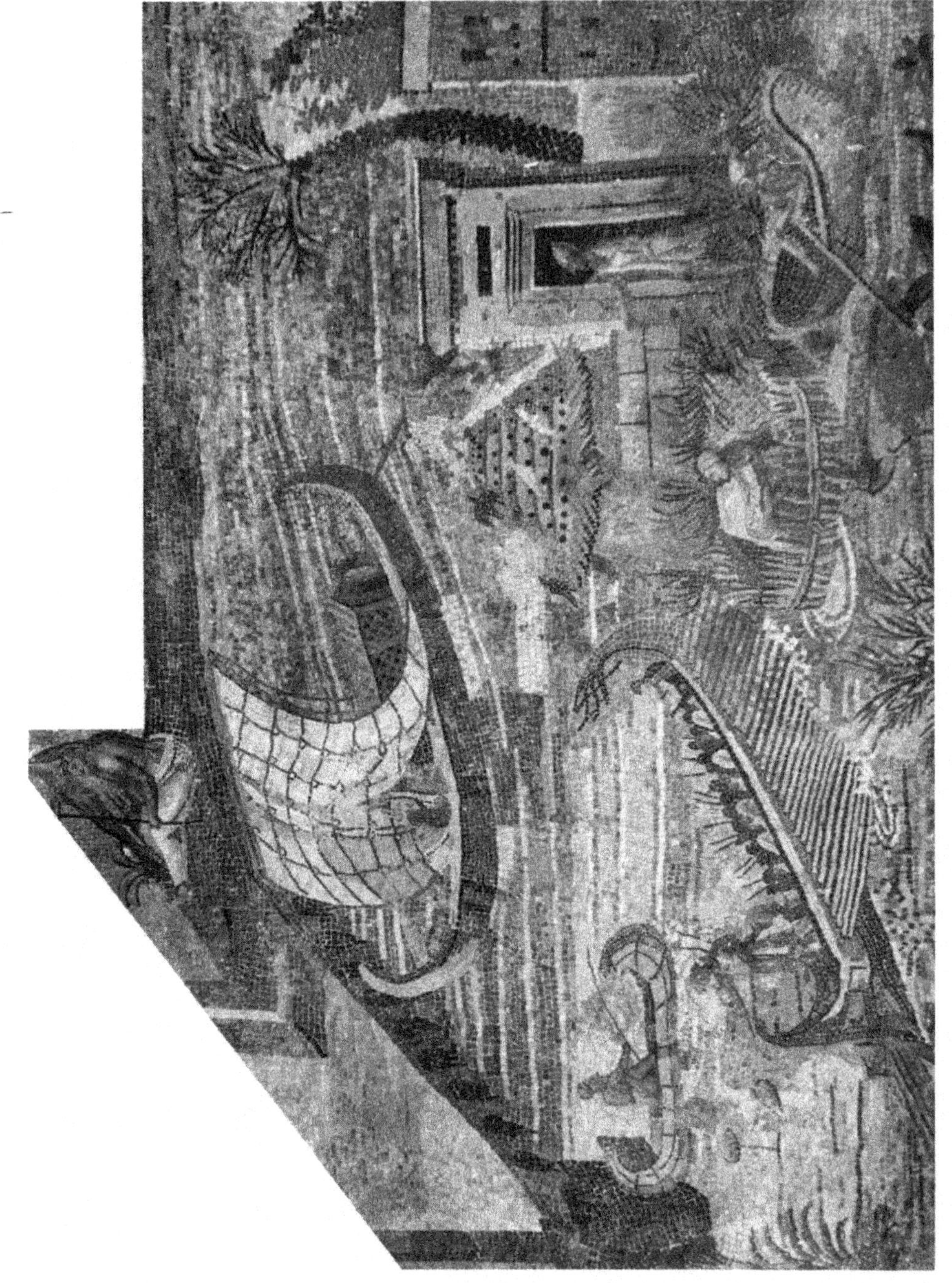

17b. The mosaic, section 17

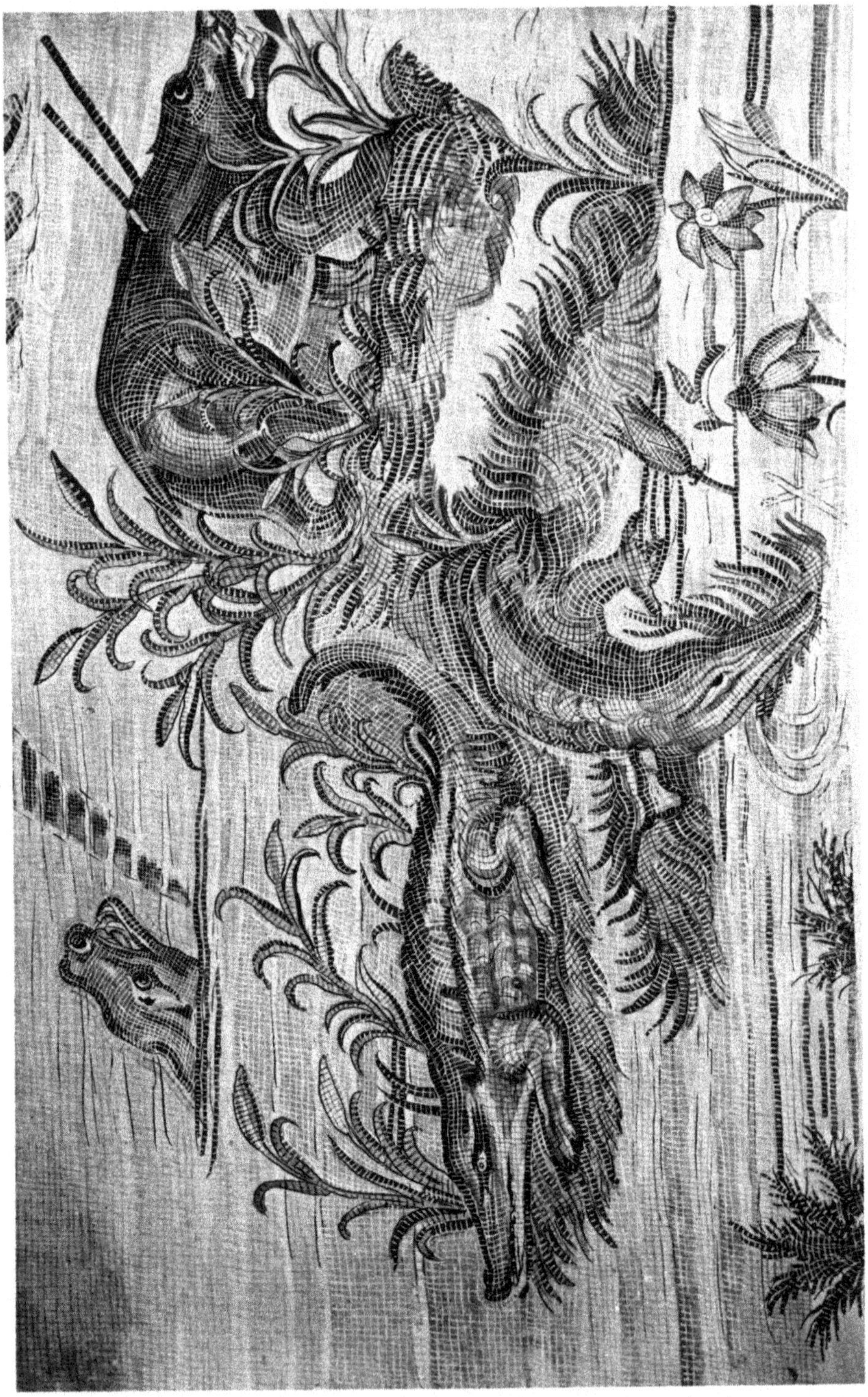

18a. Windsor drawing 19218

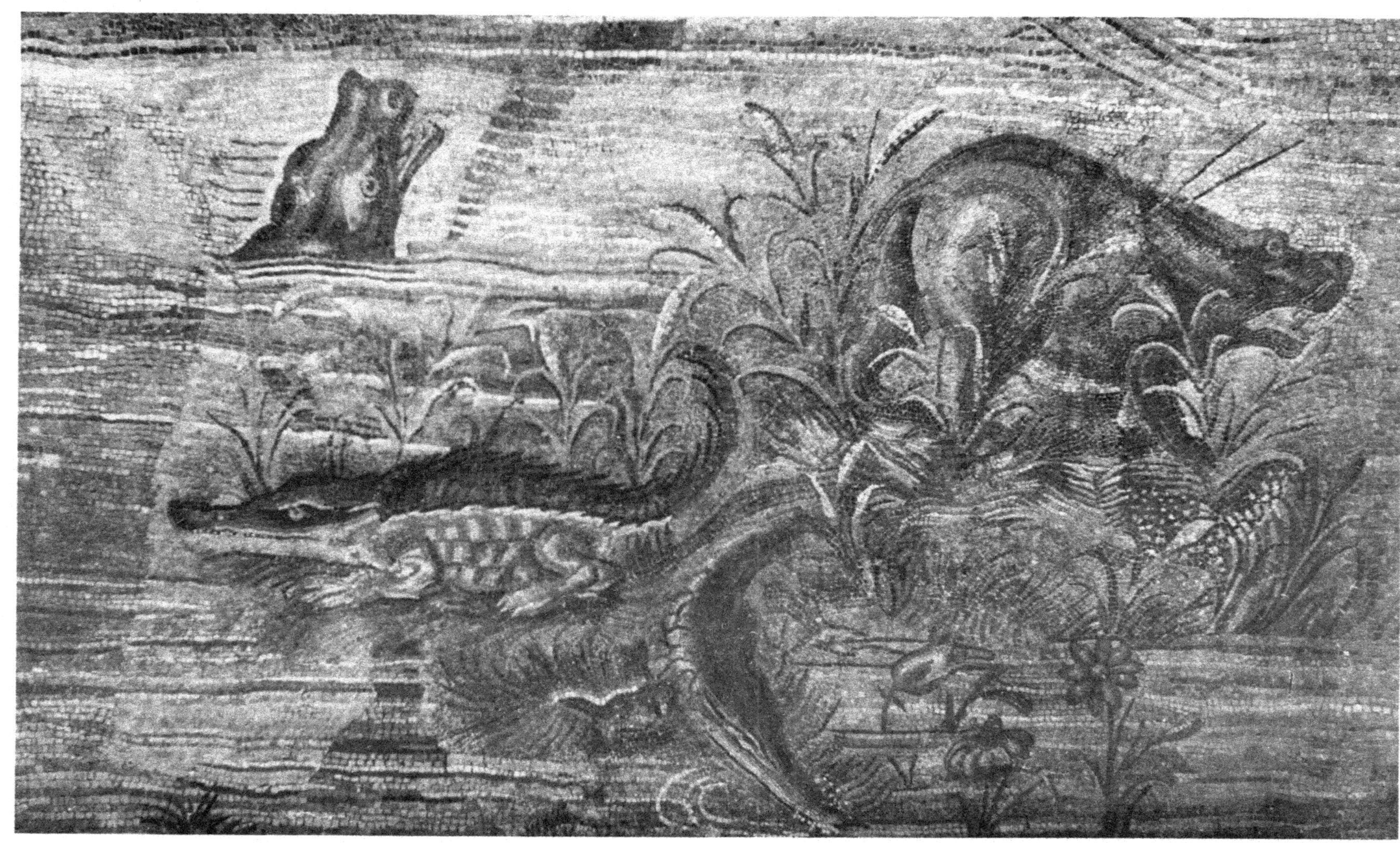

18b. The mosaic, section 18

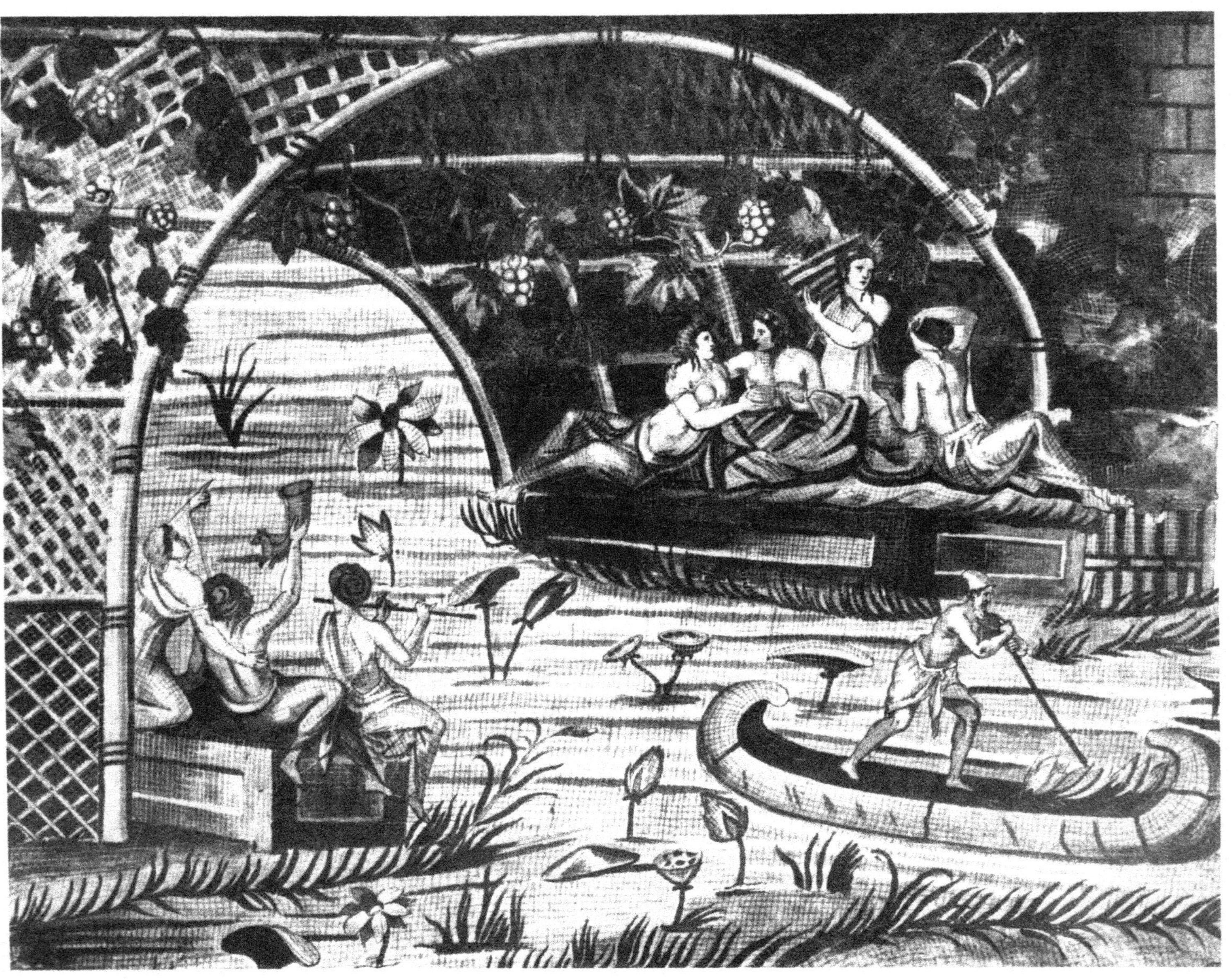

19a. Windsor drawing 19219

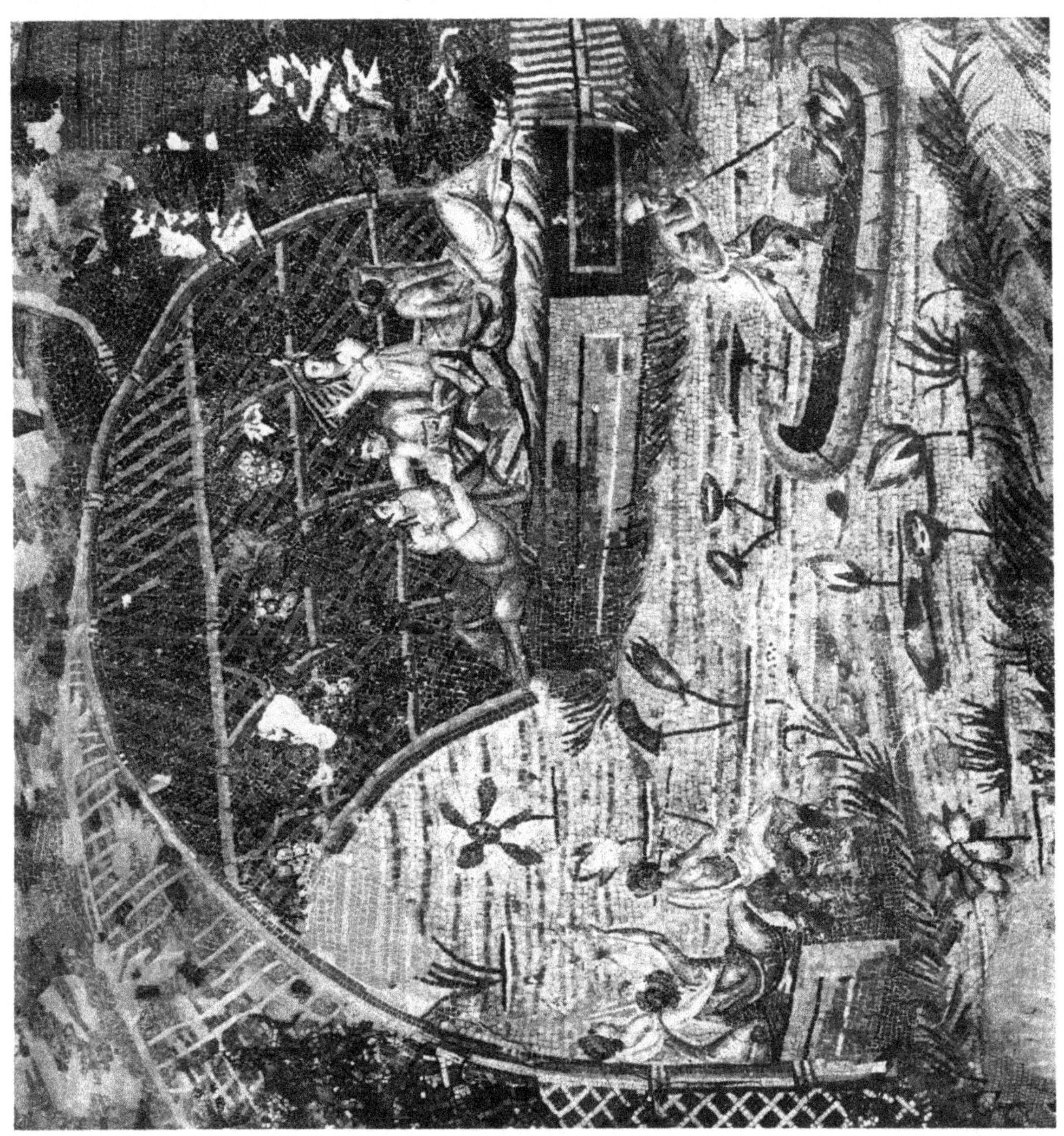

19b. The Berlin fragment of the mosaic

19c. The mosaic, section 19

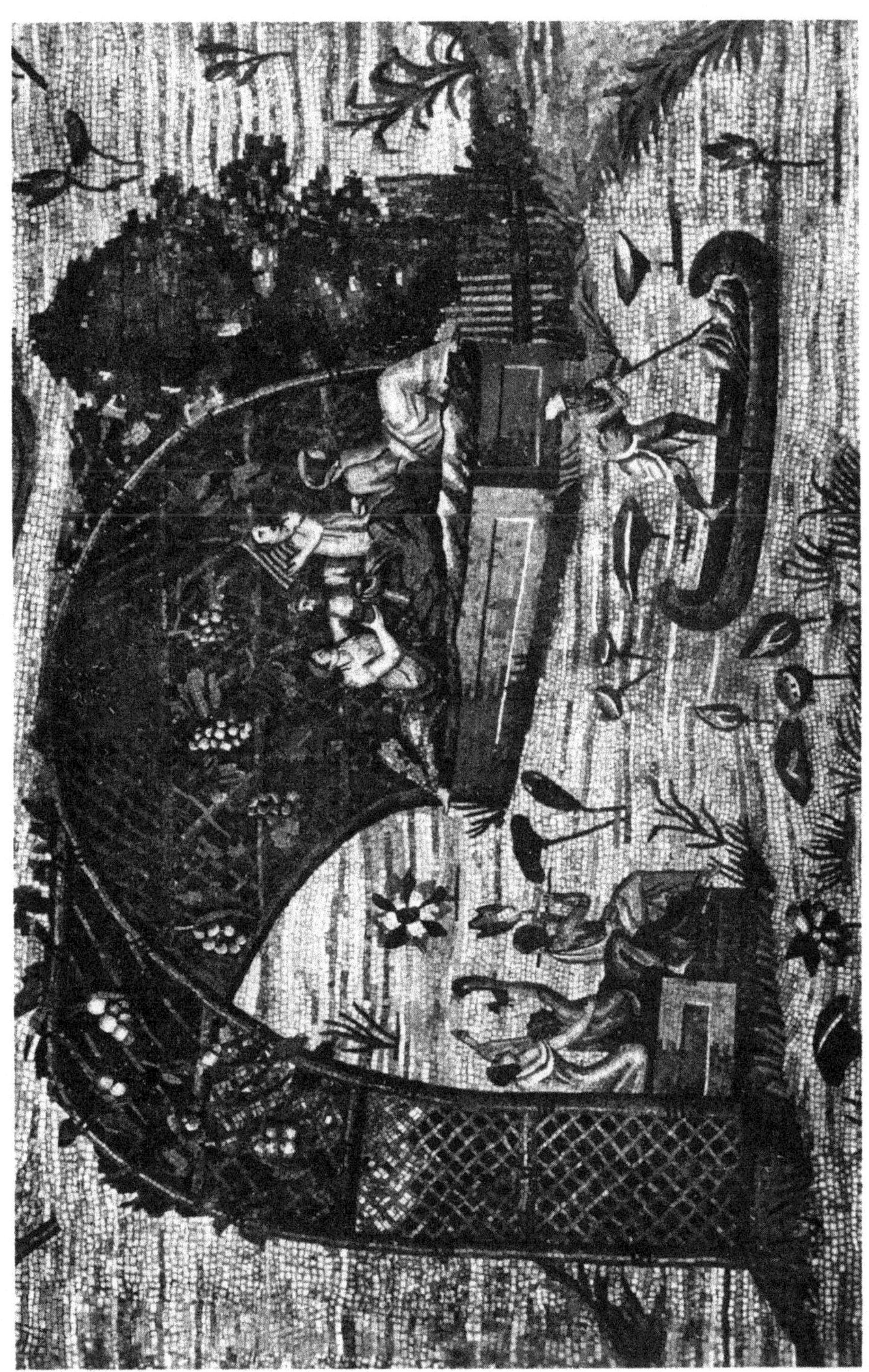

III

RECONSTRUCTION OF THE MOSAIC

The fact that the Dal Pozzo copies do not show the mosaic in one piece as found does not nullify their value as an aid in attempting to reconstruct it. They are a sufficiently faithful transcription of the original on which to base suggested alterations of its present form, and the very evidence which they present of its fragmentary state shows us how necessary a reconsideration of the seventeenth-century restorers' work is. I should like to conclude this monograph with a short examination of the possibilities which they suggest.

The accuracy with which the artist copied the blocks of mosaic before him seems on the whole to have been high. Discrepancies such as the non-appearance of the simpulum in no. 13, or the adjusted perspective and simplification of the shading in no. 8 may warn us not to place complete confidence in details; fragmentary mosaic is not the easiest form of pictorial art to decipher and copy, and his eye may have processed the material to a certain extent, rationalising the obscure and omitting the unfamiliar. However, when it is possible to check the contents of the watercolours against sections of the mosaic which have not undergone radical restoration, notably nos. 8, 12,18 and in particular no. 19, the copies are seen to be a good transcription of the original.

Comparison with restored areas of the mosaic, however, raises doubts about the part which they played in its restoration. In spite of the recorded tradition that they were followed by Calandra and his fellow workers, divergences like the disappearance of the name ϹΑΤΤΥΟϹ in no. 7, or the appearance of the letters ΞΙϘΙΓ in no. 2 imply otherwise; the senseless omission of the fourth figure in no. 16 indicates some lack of thought on the mosaicists' part, but most important, the treatment of the scene shown in no. 1 as two separate pieces suggests that if these copies were employed then they were not relied upon to any great extent. It may be that it was not this set but a less accurate one, possibly drawings belonging to Cardinal Barberini,[1] which provided the foundation for the work, but this was subsequently forgotten because the Dal Pozzo copies were well known and the first to spring to mind in connection with the mosaic. More likely, perhaps, the fact that they did not give an overall view of the mosaic might have minimized their usefulness in the eyes of the restorers, who preferred to work according to their own ideas of how the pieces fitted together with only passing reference to the drawings and not too much interest in the finer details.

If nothing else, the Dal Pozzo watercolours demonstrate that the mosaic at the time of its discovery had many missing areas, as has its opposite number, the Fish Mosaic, now.[2] Three blocks of linked scenes can be built up from the copies: two fairly large areas, that made up of nos. 6, 7, 10 and 11, with a gap in the middle, and that shown by nos. 8, 12 and 18; and one lesser, made up of nos. 1, 2 and 4. At the time of removal these were evidently cut up into smaller, more portable sections, and other single pieces were taken out as well - at least three pieces are entirely free-floating (nos. 3, 15 and 19) and bear no relation to any others, and a further two are only tentatively linked to the larger blocks (nos. 5 to 6 etc., and 9 to 10 etc.). The frequency of straight edges on the copies must indicate that fragments of mosaic were lifted by summary chopping-out or were subsequently tidied up by the removal of rough edges and loose tesserae. It seems unlikely that any record of the original pictorial scheme was kept, if only for the reasons given earlier, that the mosaic when found was not in a site conducive to copying or measuring.[3] The appearance of the numbers "2" and "4" on no. 4 and nos. 7 and 11 respectively is hard to account for; they do not correspond with the relevant numbers in Suares' list, which may show the order of the drawings in Dal Pozzo's collection, nor do they resemble the serial numbers which sometimes appear on drawings belonging to that collection. They may indicate that the fragments were numbered after their removal, or that the artist himself tried to arrange the pieces in some sort of numbered order. Whether in fact he did attempt to reassemble any fragments and draw them as one piece cannot be said for sure, but the awkward joins in nos. 11 and 13 may show that two separate pieces of mosaic were involved in either case, unless they are simply instances of his having run out of paper.

The present composition of the mosaic shows an unsatisfactory balance, with too much water to the left and too much rock to the right. Some scenes disappear off the edge - e.g. the truncated hippopotamus at the left straight side - or imply the disappearance of others: for example the group of people in no. 16 who are looking at something further right, or the dog at the bottom of no. 13 which seems to be regarding an object or figure below and right. Large blank areas of restoration hint at the absence of original figures, and the pieces occupying the lowest register have been cut off at the bottom (for instance, the stalks of the flowers in no. 19 are missing) in order to neaten the edge. It would seem that the present pictorial scheme should be dissected and a re-arrangement attempted with allowance being made for destroyed areas.

The original contours of the mosaic are unknown, its present shape being that of the seventeenth-century restoration, dictated by the form of the apse into which it was fitted in the Palazzo Barberini.[4] To achieve this form, the upper half of the mosaic was finished off around the circumference with a neat band seven to eight tesserae wide which accounts for some of the extra detail at the outer edges of pieces such as nos. 1, 4 and 7. The straight sides of the lower half were not treated thus but were merely neatened or expanded in a few places, the most notable being the right-hand side of no. 11, which is extensively padded-out. Whether the original mosaic was semi-circular or ran on into the three niches in the wall is uncertain, but it is difficult to make some of the reconstructions suggested by the drawings without allowing it a greater latitude, using some of the area of the niches. The Fish Mosaic of the "Antro delle Sorti" does follow the contours of its grotto, and I think a parallel treatment of the Nilotic example is likely.[5] Disregarding the niches, the total area which the mosaic might have occupied is 6.87 m wide and

4. 35 m maximum depth; its present size is 5. 85 m x 4. 31 m, so there is some room for re-arrangement and the hypothetical inclusion of now-vanished pieces.[6]

If the contents of the watercolours are subtracted from the present mosaic, little remains that is not fill-in restoration. The following scenes or groups of objects are original:

> the gateway behind and to right of the temple/portico in the foreground (see no. 14, p. 20, and Fig. 16b, left); the side of the tower at the right-hand side of the temple with obelisks, and the top of the tower below (see no. 8, p. 16, and Fig. 8b, right); the group of cobra, ichneumon and dog, above and to left of the temple with obelisks (Fig. 8b, top left);[7]

and were perhaps still in situ, and gathered up on the instructions of Cardinal Barberini at the time of the mosaic's restoration.[8] If their original location was noted and they were re-inserted in the mosaic accordingly, they would provide three fixed points in any attempted reconstruction, and although we cannot be sure of this it may be best to assume that these pieces are more or less where they should be; the side of the temple, no. 8, and the gateway, which follows on from no. 13 at a greater or lesser distance than at present, must be approximately correct, at least.

Some re-arrangements are made necessary by the information which the copies convey; others of a more subjective nature could be derived from the need to satisfy certain compositional demands. The mosaic seems to draw upon two sources, or more likely several sources which fall into two categories: zoological material, perhaps originally in manuscript form, for the upper part with its didactic labelling and subordination of the landscape element to the fauna, which appear as isolated units within it; and geographical, topographical or perhaps even religious material for the lower half, with its mixture of minor genre scenes and major groups of people and buildings which apparently have some particular and linked significance. A detailed examination of the possible antecedents of the mosaic forms the final part of Kyle M. Phillips's valuable thesis; for the lower half of the mosaic, dominated by "the more pictorial aspects of composes units", he follows Eva Schmidt in postulating a series of painted panels as the prototypes.[9] The differently-derived halves are united in a scheme to illustrate Egypt, or more particularly the course of the Nile, in its full extent, with the river seen at the time of its inundation - the prime season of its religious importance, a phenomenon of engrossing interest to non-Egyptian visitors and writers, and a fitting subject for a mosaic destined to spend its life under water.[10]

In contrast to the upper half, the lower displays some sense of perspective; despite its many artistic limitations, the bird's-eye-view composition shows a gradual decrease in the size of buildings and ships (though not figures) as we move up the scene. At the halfway point where the two parts merge is a zone of small-scale buildings below tracts of open water interspersed with rocky outcrops and the first of the labelled animals. Nos. 8, 9 and 10 all belong in this half-and-half register. Nos. 13, 15, 16, 18 and 19 all contain buildings of comparatively large size and belong to the lower reaches of the composition.

No. 17 seems rather small-scale by comparison and it is tempting to try to move it to a higher position, but this is made difficult by the requirements of the other pieces.

The scene shown in no. 14 should almost certainly be included at some point in the lower half of the mosaic. This will necessitate a re-arrangement involving pieces 13, 16 and 17, which comprise a progression of scenes occurring on or beside an apparently continuous causeway, the end point of which may be the purely Egyptian temple of no. 11. The series is clearly an important element and should perhaps form a more centrally-positioned unit in the picture; it must in any case move somewhat to the left because an extra scene, the object of the attention of those standing on the causeway in no. 16, has to be inserted to the right of this piece. This might be the seemingly waterside event of which the barest remnants appear in no. 14, but it is unlikely that the left-hand side of that fragment would fit here, and the artist's hypothesis that 14 should be placed next to 13 is probably correct.[11] The gateway fragment[12] would then fit above and to right of the figures whose legs and feet are visible in no. 14, and would be followed by no. 16, since the wall with merlons at the left-hand side of the latter links with the gateway. Some scene must be inserted to the right of no. 16, probably a religious ceremony on a par with those depicted in nos. 13 and 16, and almost certainly taking place on the water.[13] At the top left-hand corner of no. 15 is a small portion of the stern(?) of a boat, implying that enough space should be allowed at the left of this piece to account for a section of the original composition containing one of the larger boats, similar to that appearing at the join between nos. 10 and 11. This might be part of what is happening beside no. 16, and the two pieces could be placed adjacent to each other with a fair-sized gap in between. As remarked earlier, it would be more satisfactory for perspective if no. 17 could be fitted in higher up in the mosaic, with the vertical surface pierced by arches which just appears at the top left of the drawing forming the side of the causeway extending from 13 to 16 and perhaps beyond. The presence of an obtrusive platform to the right of this arcaded wall, however, limits the possibilities; it seems unlikely that the piece could be slotted into the diagonal axis between nos. 16 and 11, where it might seem well fitted by the relative size of its contents, because the temple in no. 11 stands on a platform (the whole of which is shown in the copy) and it is improbable that there would be a second such below. An alternative position is to the right of no. 13, allowing a gap for no. 14's inclusion,[14] where the wall would form the side of the causeway at this point and the platform above would link up with the ground on which the kiosk stands in no. 16.[15] Finally in this lower right-hand quarter of the mosaic, the fragment shown in copy no. 19 might be placed in the corner with sufficient space around it for the extra greenery which is apparently necessary.

At the left-hand side of no. 13 the walled complex above the temple in the foreground is probably incorrectly restored (see above, p. 19) and misplaced below the rustic buildings; it might belong higher up in the picture, since it stands on rock as opposed to marshy ground, or alternatively it should move to the left, where the piece of rock seen above the stern of the boat full of hippopotamus-hunters seems to be the end of the outcrop on which these buildings stand, and the tower above, of which only the top is original, may be that which seems to be a necessary addition at the end of the crenellated wall; this join between the left-hand side of no. 13 and the right of no. 8 is almost certainly correct and further supports the tendency of no. 13 and its related pieces to move to the left, with the causeway being brought into a more central position.[16] The space above no. 13 might be occupied by no. 9, treating this as a separate "floating" piece not directly connected with no. 10 as it now is in the mosaic. The block composed of nos. 8, 12 and 18 will remain where it is now placed in the mosaic, moving very slightly to the right to allow the hippopotamus its nose, as in the copy.

The upper half of the mosaic is composed of two large blocks (nos. 1, 2 and 4; 6, 7, 10 and 11) and two free pieces (no. 5, which may link to 6, and no. 3). It has been noted in dealing with individual drawings that some sections which are now set lower down in the mosaic seem to have occupied the sky-line in the original. Apart from the case of no. 1, where a change should almost certainly be envisaged, nos. 5 and 7 (5 possibly taking 6 etc. with it) should perhaps be brought up to the top register of the mosaic, making a total of six pieces at this upper level. The width would have to be increased correspondingly, and it would be necessary to utilise the extra space offered by the niches in order to accommodate this enlarged arrangement at sky-level. The scenic details of these pieces offer no immediate clues as to how they might be arranged within the upper half of the mosaic, nor is there much evidence for the manner in which they originally connected with the lower half of the picture. However, a link between nos. 10 and 16 might be tentatively urged from some minor details in the copies: the patch of vegetation vaguely sketched in at the bottom of no. 10, below the rustic hut, could be the outer edge of the leaves of the trees at the top left of no. 16. If this join were made, then the line of grass or reed just appearing top right above the kiosk in no. 16 might be part of the clump of greenery at the extreme left-hand side of the ground on which the temple stands in no. 11. This would anchor the whole block at the right-hand side of the composition and complete the diagonal progression of buildings in nos. 13, 16 and 11. The remaining pieces in the upper part would then be located in the left-hand side: no. 3 might be placed to the right of no. 1, linked perhaps by the figures of hunters moving right. The tract of land which begins to appear at the bottom left-hand corner of no. 4 might be the termination of the land behind the temple in no. 8, and the small fragment showing the cobra, ichneumon and dog[17] might be placed to the left of it, though this small piece could easily go elsewhere; at any rate, it seems certain that there should be a figure for the dog to turn and look at, and what should be supplied is perhaps an Ethiopian hunter similar to those with the dog in no. 3.

The re-arrangement of the mosaic thus arrived at (Fig. 20) results in an upper panorama composed of rocky masses projecting against sky or water, and a lower, more schematized landscape with architectural elements arranged in a diagonal plane across the picture, a device which is not without parallel in Roman landscape painting where the employment of a system of oblique perspective frequently results in a composition with a markedly diagonal flow which to modern eyes looks strangely un-centralised. The inclusion of more labelled animals in the gaps in the upper half should be envisaged, and more fill-in details in the lower half, plus the missing scene of no. 14.

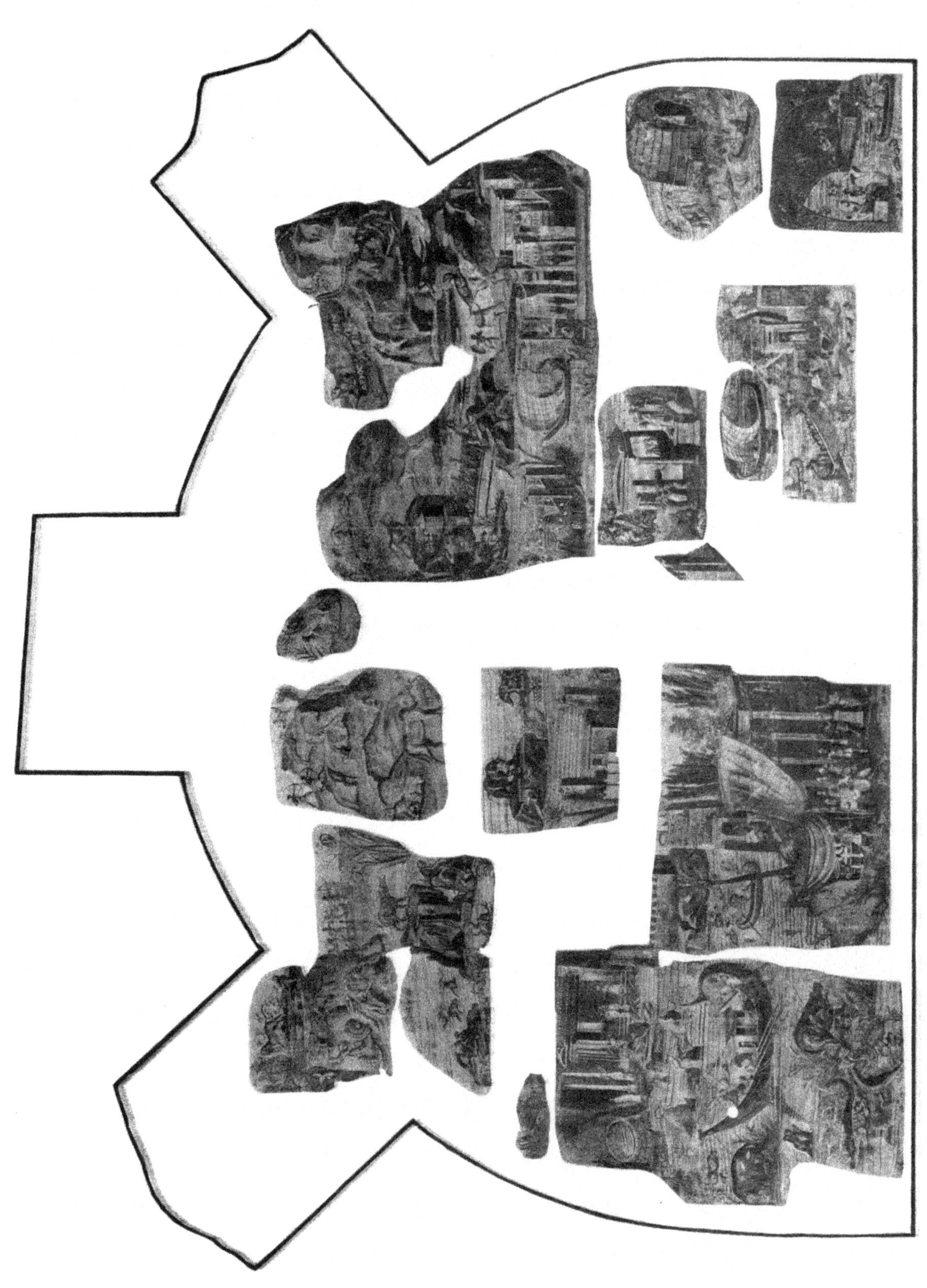

20. Suggested reconstruction of the mosaic

This is merely one attempt to utilise the information which can be derived from the copies, and other hypothetical restorations might be proposed on the basis of their contents. The reliability of the testimony which the Dal Pozzo copies afford is, of course, crucial to any such attempted reconstruction. It is hoped that this discussion of them has helped to demonstrate that they may be employed with confidence, and with profit, in a re-consideration of the Palestrina mosaic, for there is much that they can tell us about the original form of this important work. With their emergence from obscurity they may prove to be of continuing value for scholarship - a fact which would doubtless please that generous and devoted antiquary among whose "reconditos thesauros ....quos exihibet liberaliter" they were once to be found.[18]

NOTES

Chapter I

1. Thomas Shaw Travels or Observations relating to several parts of Barbary and the Levant (2nd ed., London 1757) p. 437.

2. The most recent study devoted to the mosaic is that of Giorgio Gullini, I Mosaici di Palestrina (Archeologia Classica, vol. supp. I, Rome, 1956), hereafter referred to as Gullini 1956. An earlier monograph which deals with the mosaic's contents in exhaustive but not always accurate detail is Eva Schmidt's Studien zum Barberinischen Mosaik in Palestrina (Zur Kunstgeschichte des Auslandes, 127, Strassburg, 1929), hereafter Schmidt 1929. A bibliography of early, pre-1879 references to the mosaic may be found in G. Lumbroso's L'Egitto dei Greci e dei Romani (2nd ed., Rome, 1895), pp. 14-15, n. 4. I have made extensive use for this monograph of Kyle M. Phillips's detailed and informative thesis The Barberini Mosaic: Sunt Hominum Animaliumque Complures Imagines (Princeton University, 1962; unpublished), hereafter Phillips 1962.

3. A detailed description of the apsidal building may be found in R. Delbrueck Hellenistische Bauten in Latium, I (Strassburg, 1907), pp. 77-90 (for the area in general, see pp. 47ff.); II (1912), pp. 1-4, and an attempted reconstruction, Taf. 1. For an alternative reconstruction of the exterior see: H. Hörmann "Die Fassade des Apsidensaales im Heiligtum der Fortuna zu Praeneste", R.M. 40, 1925, pp. 241-79; and for the whole town, H. Chalton Bradshaw "Praeneste: a Study for its Restoration", P.B.S.R. 9, 1920, pp. 233-62 and pls. XXVII-XXXVI, with a useful bibliography of proposed reconstructions of the temple from Giuliano da Sangallo on, pp. 244-7.

4. See Gullini 1956, pp. 20-32. The appellation "Antro delle Sorti" is derived from Cicero's account of the miraculous origin of the oracular shrine at Praeneste (de Divinatione II, 41, 85ff.): obeying a divine command, Numerius Suffustius struck the rock face and the first sortes sprang forth.

5. A resumé of the arguments concerning the temple may be found in: G. Jacopi Il Santuario della Fortuna Primigenia e il Museo Archeologico Prenestino (Itinerari dei Musei, Gallerie e Monumenti d'Italia, 100, Rome, 1959), pp. 10-13; see also H. Besig in RE Suppl. VIII (1956), "Praeneste", col. 1243ff. More particularly, see: F. Fasolo and G. Gullini Il Santuario della Fortuna Primigenia a Palestrina (Rome, 1953) and the review of it by H. Kähler in Gnomon 30, 1958, pp. 366-83; idem "Das Fortunaheiligtum von Palestrina Praeneste", Annales Universitatis Saraviensis 7, 1958, pp. 189-240; H. von Heintze "Das Heiligtum der Fortuna Primigenia in Präneste, dem heutigen Palestrina",

Gymnasium 63, 1956, pp. 526-44; and for the dating, A. Degrassi "Epigraphica IV", Mem. Linc: ser. 8, XIV, 1969-70, pp. 111-27. Gullini has replied to his critics in "La datazione e l'inquadramento stilistico del santuario della Fortuna Primigenia a Palestrina", Aufstieg und Niedergang der Römischen Welt I, 4 (Berlin/New York, 1973), pp. 746-99.

6. See the plan, Delbrueck op.cit., I, Taf. XV.

7. It was pointed out by P. Mingazzini ("Note di Topografia Prenestina. L'Ubicazione dell'Antro delle Sorti", Archeologia Classica 6, 1954, pp. 295-301) that the dampness of the "Antro delle Sorti" would disqualify it as the site of the famous oracle (see above, n. 4), and following Vaglieri ("Preneste e il Suo Tempio della Fortuna", Bull. Com. 37, 1909, 212-74) he identified the whole lower complex as a secular area, and the two mosaic-paved grottoes as nymphaea. This identification has been seconded by Kähler op.cit., "Das Fortuna-heiligtum ....", pp. 95-7, who sees the two nymphaea as a practical solution to the problem of water seepage. The possibility that the "Antro delle Sorti" could be a nymphaeum was accepted by Gullini in his Guida del Santuario della Fortuna Primigenia a Palestrina (Rome, 1956), p. 11, where he nonetheless maintained the idea of the area's specific religious purpose. For discussions of the "Antro delle Sorti" in the context of artificially elaborated nymphaea, see N. Neuerburg L'Architettura delle Fontane e dei Ninfei nell'Italia Antica (Memorie dell'Accademia di Archeologia, Lettere e Belle Arti di Napoli, V, Naples, 1965), pp. 171-3, nos. 97-8; F. B. Sear The Origins and Development of Roman Wall and Vault Mosaics (Ph.D. thesis, Cambridge University, 1971-2) pp. 85-6, no. 3.

8. Himerius Or. XLVIII, 9 (ed. Colonna): ἴδοις ἄν, ἴδοις καὶ τὰ μεγάλα τότε κατὰ τὴν ἐκεῖσε χώραν θαύματα· ἐπὶ μιᾶς γῆς πλωτῆρα τὸν αὐτὸν καὶ γηπόνον, καὶ νεμομένας βοῦς καὶ μετ᾽ ὀλίγον ὁλκάδας, καὶ νῆσον ἐξαίφνης τὴν πρόσθεν πόλιν χερσεύουσαν.

9. cf. P. H. von Blanckenhagen's observations on the correspondence between the "symbolic" class of landscape representation to which he assigns the mosaic, and the Yellow Frieze from the Casa di Livia: "The Odyssey Frieze", R.M. 70, 1963, pp. 100-46, especially p. 129.

10. Its Alexandrian quality has been stressed most recently by J. Charbonneaux, R. Martin and F. Villard in Hellenistic Art (London, 1973) pp. 177-82. The case for a Hellenistic Greek origin for landscape depiction and a specifically Alexandrian one for Nilotica has been stated most emphatically by M. Swindler Ancient Painting (New Haven, 1929) p. 318; but for an alternative view see C. M. Dawson Romano-Campanian Mythological Landscape Painting (Yale Classical Studies IX, New Haven, 1944) particularly pp. 40-41. The mosaic has been described as the sort of cartographic work of which the painter Demetrios Topographos of the second century B.C. must have been an exponent: see P. H. von Blanckenhagen and C. Alexander The Paintings from Boscotrecase (R.M. Ergänzungsheft 6, Heidelberg, 1962) pp. 55-7.

The name of this shadowy figure of apparently Alexandrian connections has often been linked with the genre of Nilotic landscapes — see, e.g., Swindler op.cit., loc.cit. and pp. 306-7; C. R. Morey Early Christian Art (Princeton, 1942) p. 143, and the review of it by D. Tselos in A.J.A. 47, 1943, pp. 144-8, particularly 146; and Martin Robertson A History of Greek Art (Cambridge, 1975) I, p. 589.

11. Datings as follows: a) Sullan, c. 80 B.C.: Delbrueck op.cit., I, pp. 47-50; Fasolo-Gullini op.cit., pp. 312ff.; G. Lugli "Il Santuario della Fortuna Primigenia in Preneste e la sua datazione", Rend. Linc. ser. 8, IX, 1954, pp. 74-5; Gullini 1956, pp. 11ff.; G.-Ch. Picard R.A. 1960, 2, p. 30 n. 3; P. F. Tschudin Isis in Rom (Aarau, 1962) p. 15; I. Lavin "The Hunting Mosaics of Antioch and their sources", Dumbarton Oaks Papers 17, 1963, pp. 223-4; P. Romanelli Palestrina (Cava dei Tirreni, Naples, 1967) pp. 69-70. Contra the Sullan dating: Kähler Gnomon 30, 1958, pp. 370-1; no alternative date proposed, but see E. Börsch-Supan Garten-, Landschafts- und Paradiesmotive im Innenraum (Berlin, 1967) p. 352 n. 294. b) 60-50 B.C.: H. G. Beyen Pompejanische Wanddekoration II, 1 (The Hague, 1960) p. 314 n. 2. c) post-30 B.C.: Jacopi op.cit., p. 23; D. Bonneau La Crue du Nil, divinité égyptienne (Paris, 1964) p. 91; cf. M. Malaise Inventaire préliminaire des documents égyptiens découverts en Italie (E.P.R.O. 21, Leiden, 1972) p. 96 no. 4. d) Hadrianic: R. van Deman Magoffin A study of the topography and municipal history of Praeneste (Baltimore, 1908) pp. 49-50; O. Marucchi "Il Grande Mosaico Prenestino ed il 'Lithostroton' di Silla" Diss. P.A.R.A. ser. 2, X, 1, 1910, pp. 167-8; Schmidt 1929, pp. 11ff.; A. Garcia y Bellido Arte Romano (Madrid, 1955) pp. 457, 460; H. von Heintze op.cit., p. 537; L. Castiglione "Griechisch-ägyptische Studien: Beiträge zur Deutung des Mosaiks von Präneste", Acta Antiqua A.S.H. 5, 1957, p. 220. e) third century A.D.: A. Rumpf Handbuch der Archäologie 4.1, Malerei und Zeichnung der Klassischen Antike (Munich, 1953) p. 193; followed by S. Morenz Die Begegnung Europas mit Ägypten (Berlin, 1968) pp. 119-20.

12. Pliny Natural History XXXVI, 64, 189.

13. The identification of the mosaic with Sulla's lithostroton was accepted by Delbrueck op.cit., I, p. 50, has been argued for at length by Gullini 1956, pp. 9ff. and Appendix pp. 51-3 (cf. Aufstieg und Niedergang der Römischen Welt, I, 4, pp. 752-60), and is admitted by many who follow his dating. That the term can be used for opus tessellatum has been asserted by H. Stern "Origine et débuts de la mosaique murale", Études d'Archéologie classique II, 1959 (Annales de l'Est publiés par la faculté des lettres de l'Université de Nancy, Memoire no. 22) p. 102 and n. 5; and although T. Dohrn (R.M. 72, 1965, pp. 127-41, particularly 132) defined "Crustae" as "Marmorplättchen" he apparently accepted the mosaic's equivalence with the Sullan lithostroton. But the latter has been defined as opus sectile by A. Tschira "Pavimenta", R.M. 55, 1940, pp. 27-35; D. Gioseffi "La terminologia dei sistemi di pavimentazione marmorea e una pagina della Naturalis Historia" Rend. Linc. ser. 8, X, 1955, pp. 572-95, particularly 575ff.; G. Becatti Scavi di Ostia IV:

Mosaici e Pavimenti Marmorei (Rome, 1961), pp. 253-67; and Ph. Bruneau "Deux noms antiques de pavement, ΚΑΤΑΚΛΥΣΤΟΝ et ΛΙΘΟΣΤΡΩΤΟΝ", Bulletin de Correspondance Hellénique 91, pp. 423-46, particularly 431ff. For the view that the mosaic could not be the Sullan lithostroton see, inter aliis, Marucchi op.cit., pp. 157-65, and others cited therein; Schmidt 1929, p. 10; von Heintze op.cit., p. 537; Kähler Gnomon 30, p. 382; Beyen op.cit., p. 3 n. 3.

14. A. Maiuri La villa dei Misteri (Rome, 1931) pp. 197-9 and Fig. 83; H. G. Beyen Pompejanische Wanddekoration I (The Hague, 1938) p. 55; W. J. T. Peters Landscape in Romano-Campanian Mural Painting (Assen, 1963) p. 8.

15. E. Pernice Die Hellenistische Kunst in Pompeji, VI: Pavimente und Figürliche Mosaiken (Berlin, 1938) pp. 167-8 and Taf. 68, 1-4; K. Schefold Vergessnes Pompeji (Bern, 1962) pp. 17, 197.

16. The comparison between the mosaic and the Odyssey Frieze was first drawn by G. Cultrera Saggi sull'arte ellenistica e greco-romana I (Rome, 1917) pp. 232-4, and has been elaborated on by A. Gallina "Le pitture con paesaggi dell'Odissea dall'Esquilino", Studi Miscellanei 6, 1960-61, pp. 39-41; see also L. Vlad Borrelli Bollettino d'Arte 41, 1956, pp. 297-8, and Beyen op.cit., II, 1, pp. 312-5. A warning note on their comparability has however been sounded by von Blanckenhagen op.cit., especially pp. 112, 129, 144.

17. cf. the examples in nn. 14 and 15 above. The appearance of Isiac symbols as control marks on Roman coins of the first half of the first century B.C. must indicate a degree of popular familiarity with this material (but surely not the religious affiliations of the mint workers, as suggested by A. Alföldi "Isiskult und Umsturzbewegung im letzten Jahrhundert der römischen Republik", Schweizer Münzblätter 5, 1954, Heft 18, pp. 25-31; cf. Malaise op.cit., p. 238ff. and M. H. Crawford Roman Republican Coinage, Cambridge, 1974, I, pp. 399, 439; II, p. 584 n. 2). For the assimilation of Fortuna with Isis at Palestrina and the resulting presence of Egyptian material there, see E. Köberlein Caligula und die Ägyptischen Kulte (Beiträge zur Klassischen Philologie, Heft 3, Meisenheim am Glan, 1962) pp. 70-71, and cf. K. Schefold "Zur hellenistischen Theologie Alexandrias", ΑΝΤΙΔΩΡΟΝ Edgar Salin zum 70 Geburtstag (Tübingen, 1962) pp. 167-81. At a later date the occurrence of Egyptianising material at Palestrina may also be explained by Hadrian's residence there, see below n. 20.

18. Beyen — see n. 11, b).

19. D. Bonneau op.cit., pp. 90-94, stressing the fact that Augustus' visit of 30 B.C. was associated with a particularly abundant flood; further, she has identified the temple scene with soldiers in the foreground as the emperor's arrival at Alexandria with his praetorian guard (distinguished by their scorpion-emblazoned shields) and a Roman boat, the liburnica, offshore. An earlier identification of this vessel as a Roman type, a bireme, was made by F. Moll Das Schiff in der Bildenden Kunst (Bonn, 1929) p. 29.

20. Hadrian restored an imperial villa at Palestrina (Besig *op.cit.*, 1255, 38ff.) and this may have contained Egyptianising works of art on a par with those at Tivoli, whence the fashion could have spread to the town itself; so material of this sort might not be attributable exclusively to the influence of the temple. The one Nilotic mosaic datable with any certainty to the Hadrianic period, that which forms part of the pavement signed by Heraklitos, from the Vigna Lupi on the Aventine, Rome (now in the Vatican, Museo Gregoriano Profano: B. Nogara *I mosaici antichi conservati nei palazzi pontifici del Vaticano e del Laterano*, Milan, 1910, pp. 3-5 and Tavv. V-VII) seems to me to be composed in a spirit quite different to that of the Palestrina example but perfectly in keeping with other Egyptianising works of its period, which betray a selective approach aimed at the re-creation of a fancied milieu rather than a real one such as the Palestrina mosaic presents.

21. For a summary of the early identifications see K. Woermann *Die Landschaft in der Kunst der alten Völker* (Munich, 1876) pp. 304-6; Woermann himself favoured no specific identifications but thought that the figures were stock types.

22. E.g. the Egyptian temple top right has been taken for the great temples of Karnak, Luxor or Edfu; the well and temple at the left-hand side for the Nilometer at Elephantine and the temple of Isis on the island of Philae, or for Hermopolis and the well at Tuna el-Gebel; the foreground area for Canopus, Alexandria or Memphis. See, for instance: Schmidt 1929, pp. 33ff.; Bonneau *op.cit.*, pp. 91-4; S. Aurigemma "Il restauro di consolidamento del Mosaico Barberini, condotto nel 1952", *Rend. P.A.R.A.* ser. III, 30-31, 1957-9, pp. 41-98, especially pp. 57, 59, 69, 75-7; R. E. Witt *Isis in the Graeco-Roman World* (London, 1971) pp. 34-5 and 163-4. The entire picture was taken as a representation of Elephantine and linked to Hadrian's visit there in 131 A.D. by the Abbé Barthélemy in his *Explication de la mosaique de Palestrine* (Paris, 1760). For a discussion of the architecture in general and its relation to actual Egyptian buildings, see M. I. Rostovtzeff "Die hellenistisch-römische Architekturlandschaft", *R.M.* 26, 1911, pp. 60-62.

23. cf. M. I. Rostovtzeff *The Social and Economic History of the Hellenistic World* (Oxford, 1953) p. 318.

24. Blake M.A.A.R. 8, 1930, p. 141.

25. cf. nn. 14 and 15 above.

26. E.g.: the lotus *nelumbium nuciferum*, seen *passim* in the mosaic, bears pink flowers and broad bell-shaped leaves on long stalks clear of the water. The plant seems to have come into Egypt from India some time after 1000 B.C., perhaps post the Persian conquest; it never appears in Pharaonic art, but its distinctive seed-head is represented on a purely Egyptian relief which may be dated any time between 300 to 30 B.C.: see H. Schäfer "Ein griechisch-ägyptisches Relief", *Berliner Museen: Berichte aus den Preuszischen Kunstsammlungen* 42, 1920-21, pp. 15-22, especially p. 16. It is shown in its botanically correct form in the Casa del Fauno Nilotic mosaic (above, n. 15), where it is

clearly distinguished from the lotus of the Nymphaea species, the leaves of which float on the surface of the water; in a fragment of Nilotic mosaic from Rome (M. E. Blake M.A.A.R. 17, 1940, pl. 20, fig. 3 and p. 104 — see Chap. III, n. 13); in the Palestrina mosaic; and slightly less correctly in a Pompeian mosaic emblema showing ducks and lotus (from the Casa del Cinghiale: Pernice op.cit., pp. 168-9 and Taf. 69, 1) which is probably contemporaneous with the Casa del Fauno mosaics. Elsewhere its depiction suffers from a steady degeneration, reaching its nadir (well documented by S. Aurigemma I Mosaici di Zliten, Africa Italiana, II, Rome, 1926, pp. 119ff., n. 11) in North African mosaics of the third century A.D.

27. For instance, some of the agricultural labourers shown in the mosaic appear in working dress consisting of a short belted tunic and a pointed cap. There is no parallel for them elsewhere in extant Roman Nilotic scenes, where there are in fact no straightforward representations of ordinary Egyptians at work, but they are close relatives of the peasants shown working in the fields on the walls of the tomb of Petosiris at Hermopolis (G. Lefebvre Le Tombeau de Petosiris, Cairo, 1924, III, pls. XII-XV). The tomb is dated c. 325-300 B.C. and the wall-paintings seem to have been executed by Egyptians under Greek influence, for they display side by side religious set-pieces following the conventions of Pharaonic art and scenes of daily life which betray the impact of Greek principles of rendering form or may even in some cases derive wholly from Greek sources — see H. Schäfer and W. Andrae Die Kunst des alten Orients[3] (Propyläen-Kunstgeschichte 2, Berlin, 1942) pp. 120-1, and W. Stevenson Smith The Art and Architecture of Ancient Egypt (Harmondsworth, 1958) pp. 252-3. For observations on the peculiar hat, which also appears on the relief cited above, n. 26, see Schäfer op.cit., p. 16.

28. A description of it appears in a miscellany of documents dated between those years in the archives of Palestrina: D. Sante Pieralisi Osservazioni sul musaico di Palestrina (Rome, 1858) p. 12.

29. Pieralisi op.cit.

30. Pieralisi ibid., p. 3.

31. ". . . Exstantis modo lithostroti exemplum habeas, cuius occasione Praenestinae ipsius Fortunae frontem habuisti. In eo multa quidem perspicienda sunt, quae lapillorum interrasis miculis, crustulisque intercisis, superstitiosa sedulitate, summoque otii dispendio conficta apparent. Loco in ipso nonnisi accensis facibus, superaffusaque ad perspicuitatem aqua, et saepe iterata inspersione pervidere expingereque licuit. Sunt hominum animaliumque complures imagines; Elephas Rhinoceros, nomina litteris quibusdam peculiaribus exscripta. Sunt et in aquis navigia, quae singillatim summa cum diligentia depicta apud doctrina simul ac nobilitate praeclarum Equitem Cassianum de Puteo Lincaeum collegam nostrum spectare poteris." (Pieralisi ibid., p. 3 n. 1)

32. "senza essersene preso pianta o disegno" see below, n. 35, for the source of this quotation.

33. "Il Palazzo del Vescovo sotto sue viscere haveva il famoso musaico poco fa spicconato con molto disgusto di tutti li cittadini" — a manuscript in the Barberini archives among documents relating to the sale of the feud: Pieralisi op.cit., p. 8.

34. See below, n. 19, pp. 23-4.

35. ". . . qual pezzo da una copia che si fece far a olio esattissima da Vincenzo, et è in casa, il cardinale Barberino lo fece rifar da Giovan Battista Calandra vercellese intendentissimo del lavoro di mosaico, qual raccommodò gli altri pezzi di detto mosaico, e riportatili di ordine di detto Signor a Palestrina, unitigli insieme al meglio modo che si potè con l'aiuto di disegni di casa, lo rimesse in opra in un pavimento di stanza in detto luogo di Palestrina. Convenne al Calandra valersi nel rifare sì il detto pezzo che mancava che nel raccomodare gli altri di diverse breccie trovate nel contorno di Palestrina." Naples, Biblioteca Nazionale, cod. V.E. 10, Notizie di varie antichità con un trattato di marmi: quoted in full by G. Lumbroso " Notizie sulla vita di Cassiano dal Pozzo", Miscellanea di Storia Italiana 15, 1874, pp. 131-388 (= an offprint Notizie sulla vita di Cassiano dal Pozzo, Turin, 1875, with pagination beginning 1ff.), where this passage appears on p. 171. For details of the Naples miscellany, see ibid., p. 160; the whole section from which this passage is drawn, "Notizie di diverse anticaglie", is reproduced pp. 175-211. The account cites Magalotti, not Peretti, as responsible for having the mosaic removed to Rome, but this must be a mistake. Regarding the identity of the "Vincenzo" who made the copy, Lumbroso had two suggestions: the "M. Vincenzo Pittore" mentioned to Cassiano in a letter of 1646, or the "Vincenzo intagliatore pisano" recommended to him in 1640 (cf. Lumbroso op.cit., p. 179 n. 1).

36. An entry in the Barberini archive for that date reads: "E più ho mandato a Palestrina molte casse di musaichi antichi per ordine dell'Eminentissimo e Reverendissimo Sig. Cardinale Padrone." (Pieralisi op.cit., p. 8; cf. ibid., p. 7, a draft inscription recording the mosaic's return to Palestrina in that year.)

37. i.e. the uppermost level of the temple.

38. ". . . havendo ordinato che s'incassassero et se riponessero nel Palazzo di Palestrina, furno armate le casse a rovescio in modo, che havevano macinato et scommesso tutto il musaico; però con li disegni gia cavati dal mai abbastanza lodato Cav. Cassiano dal Pozzo et dalla lunga cura et molto peritia del . . . Calandra fu tutto riposto insieme: et havendo Taddeo Barberino tolto il semiciclo[37] . . . per l'edifitio di una sala, rimasta in quello una gran nicchia, tribuna o absida che vogliamo dire, ivi ripose il detto litostroto cosi ben ristaurato, che neppure una pietruccola vi manca o alcuna ne sia scommessa o fuori dell'antico ordine...." (Pieralisi ibid., p. 10). Pieralisi thought the author of the letter was Cardinal Barberini. An anonymous French visitor to the Palazzo in the early eighteenth century describes

seeing the mosaic in "une espece de grande niche, dont la voute soutient les deux rampes separées, par lesquelles on monte au premier palier du principal escalier de ce bâtiment" — quoted by G. Turnbull A Treatise on Ancient Painting (London, 1740) p. 171, n. 24.

39. A prior restoration before the mosaic was taken back to Palestrina has been postulated, presumably on the basis of the note in the Naples manuscript (see above, n. 35), but this detail is missing from the account quoted above. The Palestrina mosaic was not the only commission which Calandra undertook for the Cardinal: he may have been responsible for restoring the apse mosaic of the Church of S. Teodoro on the Palatine during 1642-4 — see C. R. Morey Lost Mosaics and Frescoes of Rome of the Mediaeval Period (Princeton Monographs in Art and Archaeology IV, 1915) pp. 25-6.

40. Suares Praenestes Antiquae Libri Duo p. 48.

41. Pieralisi op.cit., p. 7; dated 1638.

42. Florence, 1664; ". . . a lui si dee la restaurazione del pavimento di commessi nel tempio della Fortuna fabbricato a Preneste da L. Silla, perche una parte scomposta nel di lui intero disegno si conservo" (p. 14).

43. From this restoration dates the placing of the stemma of the Barberini family on either side of the mosaic at the top; these were removed in the twentieth-century restoration.

44. S. Aurigemma 'Il restauro di consolidamento del Mosaico Barberini, condotto nel 1952", Rend. P.A.R.A. Ser. III, 30-31, 1957-9, pp. 41-98, hereafter referred to as Aurigemma 1959. Particularly useful are the diagrams indicating the areas of original mosaic compared with restoration. A similar device is employed in Gullini's plates (Gullini 1956), where the original patches are isolated and shown in conjunction with the appropriate area of the restored mosaic. Gullini's and Aurigemma's divisions do not always correspond, however, and in one or two cases both have missed small but unmistakable patches of restoration.

45. p. 6.

46. Suares' plates are extremely problematic. They are two in number, appended to the second part of his work and thus dating from 1655, and show four pieces of the mosaic, depicted with uneven edges as though they were fragments: i) the temple with soldiers in the foreground, ii) the small, walled temple complex to right of the temple with obelisks, iii) the figure of a man holding a trident standing at the side of the latter temple, and iv) the man punting a papyrus boat past a palm tree, above and to left of the temple with soldiers. In addition, at the top left-hand corner of iv) is a ragged piece showing a long-legged bird and a snail — part of one of the S. Maria in Trastevere mosaics, though Suares has said in his text (p. 291) "In Sancta Maria Transtyberim . . . fragmenta sunt duo, que Musivi Praenestini quidam suspicati sunt . . . sed illa pertinere ad aliud Musivum censent Antiquarij naris emunctioris". The plates vary considerably in large and small details from both the mosaic

and the Dal Pozzo copies (even allowing for an engraver's free interpretation and deliberate "antiquating" of them by giving them rough edges), yet in a note apparently written by Suares (Pieralisi op.cit., p. 4) with reference to expanding the edition of his work, we read: "Inserenda est musivi seu lithostroti delineatio, cuius duae figurae sunt typis expressae, reliquae apud equitem Cassianum a Puteo.". In the text itself he describes them merely as "duo ista fragmenta typis hic expressa", p. 288, though he may still be thinking of them in terms of Dal Pozzo. In the absence of the Dal Pozzo copies, the plates have sometimes been taken for engravings after them, but this is clearly not the case. Suares must have been muddled over the exact source of his illustrations. The letter quoted by Pieralisi (op.cit., pp. 9-10, quoted in part above, p. 7) congratulating Suares on the publication of his book has this to say on the subject: ". . . V.S. loda il nobile pensiero del Sig. Principe di S. Angelo Federico Cesi di restituire la forma del detto tempio. . . anzi com'egli fece incidere li fragmenti del litostroto di Silla su'rami su li quali sono impresse le due ultime carte . . . .", and this may be nearer the truth. If the plates are indeed connected with Cesi and were drawn from the mosaic in situ, they serve as ample proof that it was not possible to see it properly in its original position. They may possibly have belonged to Dal Pozzo, for in 1632 he bought some of the deceased Prince's library (see Lumbroso op.cit., p. 158). But the Windsor watercolours cannot be the models for Suares' plates; nor are they connected with the engravings which appear on the plate facing p. 190 of Nicolas Bergier's Histoire des grands chemins de l'Empire Romain I (Brussels, 1736), though these have sometimes been suggested as engravings after them. The plate shows two sections of the mosaic, corresponding to i) and iv) above, plus a third which shows the procession of priests passing through a small shrine: from details in the latter it can be proved that Bergier's sources were drawings made after the mosaic's restoration.

47. For an account of Dal Pozzo's career, see the work by Lumbroso cited above, p. 8, n. 1; also F. Haskell and S. Rinehart "The Dal Pozzo Collection, some new evidence", The Burlington Magazine 102, 1960, pp. 318-26, particularly 318-9; S. Somers-Rinehart "Poussin et la famille dal Pozzo", Nicolas Poussin (ed. Chastel) I, Paris, 1960, pp. 19ff.; idem, "Cassiano dal Pozzo (1588-1657): some unknown letters", Italian Studies 16, 1961, pp. 35ff.; C. C. Vermeule "The Dal Pozzo-Albani Drawings of Classical Antiquities", The Art Bulletin 38, 1956, pp. 31-46, particularly 31-6; idem, "Aspects of Scientific Archaeology in the seventeenth century", Proceedings of the American Philosophical Society 102, no. 2, April 1958, pp. 193-214; S. Waetzoldt Die Kopien des 17. Jahrhunderts nach Mosaiken und Wandmalereien in Rom (Veröffentlichung der Bibliotheca Hertziana 18, Vienna, 1964) pp. 14-17; A. Blunt Nicolas Poussin (Bollingen Series, New York, 1967) text, pp. 100-102.

48. Pieralisi op.cit., p. 5.

49. C. C. Vermeule "The Dal Pozzo-Albani drawings of classical antiquities in the British Museum", Transactions of the American Philosophical Society, new series, L, 5, 1960, p. 6.

50. See p. 6.

51. As hypothesised by Aurigemma 1959, pp. 95-6.

52. See A. Blunt op.cit., p. 101.

53. "Evvi finalmente il quinto, in cui veggonsi le figure del Vergilio antico, e del Terenzio della Vaticana, il Musaico del Tempio della Fortuna di Palestrina fatto da Silla, ed altre cose colorite." F. Baldinucci Cominciamento e progresso dell'arte dell'Intagliare in rame colle vite di molti de'più eccellenti Maestri della stessa professione (Florence, 1686) p. 83 = idem Notizie de'Professori del Disegno, Sec. V 1610-70 (Florence, 1728) pp. 480-79 [sic] (with minor variations of spelling, etc.).

54. A. Blunt in E. Schilling The German Drawings in the Collection of Her Majesty the Queen at Windsor Castle (London, 1971) pp. 121-2; the order described by Baldinucci no longer holds good, for the drawings were rearranged before or after their purchase (see p. 10 and n. 60) and Dal Pozzo's system of arrangement by topic was abandoned. However, his fourth folio is still recognisable, Pf. 184.

55. In his publication of a selection of these copies, C. R. Morey (op.cit. above, p. 84 n. 39) identified the artist of those with which he was dealing as Antonio Eclissi (Morey, p. 4), a view seconded by Waetzoldt, op.cit., p. 20. In his discussion of the copyists Waetzoldt adjudged that Testa was responsible for the drawings of Roman antiquities but that Dal Pozzo would have employed specialists for paintings and mosaics (p.19). Mrs. Sheila Somers Rinehart believes, on stylistic grounds, that the Palestrina copies are not the work of Testa.

56. Suares op.cit., pp. 288-91.

57. See Chap. II, drawing no. 15; on the other hand, no. 14 appears in Suares' list but has now disappeared from the mosaic.

58. Pieralisi (op.cit., p. 14) thought that Suares should have said "factum est" instead of "coeptum est", because this would fit in better with the date of composition in the 1650s. But Suares' method of composing his book seems to have been long-drawn-out and rather haphazard, and he may well have incorporated earlier notes without making appropriate amendments.

59. See John Fleming "Cardinal Albani's drawings at Windsor: their purchase by James Adam for George III", The Connoisseur 142, July-December 1958, pp. 164-9; A. Blunt in E. Schilling op.cit., pp. 8-9; C. C. Vermeule The Art Bulletin 38, 1956, pp. 34ff.; T. Ashby P.B.S.R. 6, 1913, pp. 184-5.

60. The arrangement may be that of the Albani collection, and the drawings were merely re-bound at Windsor: see Vermeule op.cit., supra, pp. 34-5.

61. Cambridge, 1882; pp. 84-5 and 718-21. The task had earlier been tackled with limited success by B. B. Woodward in The Gentleman's Magazine 1866, I, pp. 29-36: he attributed many of the Dal Pozzo drawings to Pietro Santi Bartoli (1635-1700) and his son Francesco.

62. For a list of earlier brief notices, see Michaelis ibid., p. 718; an exception is F. Matz in Göttinger Nachrichten 1872, p. 66, who mentions the Palestrina copies as being among those owned by two private collectors, Sir William Hamilton and A. W. Franks. Matz's information is not first-hand but comes via de Rossi from a letter of Lanciani's (cf. below, p. 93 n. 45), and some confusion must have arisen. A subsequent note of the Windsor drawings by Lanciani appeared in Bull. Com. 1895, pp. 168-70, and a later notice of Michaelis's in J.d.I. 25, 1910, pp. 110-26.

63. I am most grateful to the Librarian, Miss Luciana Valentini, for her help in finding the relevant papers.

64. Waetzoldt op.cit., p. 16 n. 64; Blunt op.cit., figs. 250 a-e on pp. 310-11. Apart from the post-restoration engravings of the mosaic enumerated by Pieralisi (op.cit., p. 6) at least one drawing, apparently of an isolated fragment and corresponding to no. 9 of the present set, existed and was in the possession of Dr. Richard Mead, for it is mentioned by Thomas Shaw: "In Dr. Mead's curious collection of Bartoli Drawings we see the same group of animals with the appellation ΧΟΙΡΟΠΙΘ-ΙΛ annexed to it." (op. cit. in n. 1 above, p.77). Mead seems to have purchased, either while on a grand tour of Italy in 1695-6 or later, a collection of drawings which had been in the possession of Cardinal Massimi and consisted of copies of, in the main, wall-paintings, some by Bartoli and some earlier. At the time of Mead's death it was not sold with his collection of antiquities but was retained by his family (sale catalogue, Musei Meadiani, pars altera, London, 1755, p. 112). Michaelis's identification of these drawings with a volume in the Royal Library has been questioned by Sir Anthony Blunt (The Burlington Magazine 109, 1967, pp. 31-2) and I have been unable to find any evidence for their present whereabouts, if they still exist. There is no mention of the Palestrina mosaic in the several references to Mead's collection in the works of Dr. George Turnbull.

Chapter II

1. At the time of Ashby's notes they were contained in Portfolio no. 5, which included drawings 12055-12141. I have been unable to trace this portfolio in the notices mentioned in n. 61 above but it is an interesting coincidence that it bore the same number as the libro which Baldinucci designated as containing the Vergil and Terence copies and the Palestrina mosaic (see p. 9).

2. Briefly noted by Michaelis J.d.I. 25, 1910, p. 124.

3. Suares' descriptions quoted with each drawing hereafter are to be found in Praenestes Antiquae Libri Duo pp. 289-91. They may be translated

as follows:

"In the first picture are displayed three wild animals composed of mosaic, which are inscribed ΥΛΜΟΝΟΠΑΡΔΑΛΙ perhaps ΚΑΜΕΛΟΠΑΡΔΑΛΙ.

In the second crabs swimming in the river, monkeys, a hippopotamus, hunters, and amongst these Moors, who are firing off arrows from bows at a monkey, below CΦΙΝΓΙΑ.

In the third, tortoises swimming in the river, and wild animals which are swallowing fish, and the inscription ΕΝΥΔΡΙC.

In the fourth birds, perhaps ibises sitting on a rock, and eating them a winding snake twisting its coils; a monkey, and a quadruped with human face but with a tail, and below ΜΟΝΟΚΕΝΤΑΥΡΑ, then two animals licking or biting each other, and ΘΩΑΝΤΕC added.

The fifth shows a papyrus boat being rowed along the river, which is dotted with rocks, and in it soldiers who are hurling javelins at a hippopotamus, with which they are transfixing it amidst the sedge or papyrus.

The sixth a hippopotamus run through with spears, [another] swimming, and two crocodiles.

In the seventh a ΚΡΟΚΟΔΙΛΟΠΑΡΔΑΛΙC swims in the river, and Ethiopians armed with shields hunt it; a sanctuary, statues of Isis, an eagle standard, a man mounted on an ass.*

In the eighth a ship with billowing sail heads for a round tower and two square buildings jutting out into the water, in which birds are nesting; an archer aiming at a hippopotamus.

In the ninth a temple at the river bank, obelisks, a well, a palm tree, women, assuredly, garlanded with sedge, a man holding a trident, perhaps Neptune.

In the tenth ΡΙΝΟΚΕΡΩC, ΧΟΙΡΟΠΙΟΚ, a temple with two towers, and a house, palm trees.

In the eleventh a man and a woman reclining on this side, and others further on under a pergola, which is shaded by the foliage of a vine burdened with grapes at the riverbank, and through which slips a papyrus boat full of budding flowers; on the opposite side three figures, of which one plays a reed-pipe, another stretches forth a drinking-horn or scoop which terminates in the form of a kid, the third lifts a forefinger.

In XII are to be read ΚΗΙΥΙΤΗΝ ΛΕΑΙΝΑ CΑΥΟC ΤCΗΧΙCΝΙΕ ΕΦΑΛΟC.

In XIII is to be seen a ship propelled by oars, full of soldiers, others with sails billowing in the wind and intertwined with ropes, a papyrus boat in the river, a dwelling, and a house with rustics, a skiff, and flowers in the river.

* reading "impositus" instead of "impositum".

In XIV ΚΡΟΚΟΤΑC , hunters, ΥΑΒΟΥC on a rock by the riverside.

In XV ΤΙΓΡΙC ΚΡΟΚΟΔΙΛΟC ΧΕΡCΑΙΟC CΑΤΤΙΟΚ

In XV(I) a tent; and soldiers, and a temple, a commander drinking a health with a horn, a stand full of vessels, river.

In XVII, a procession of priests beneath a temple, four garlanded ones carry a litter on their shoulders, others with tambourines and flutes; a statue of Anubis on a pedestal.

XVIII A sunshade."

Studies of the epigraphy of the mosaic may be found in: A. Böckh and J. Franz Corpus Inscriptionum Graecarum III (Berlin, 1853) pp. 858-9, no. 6131b; G. Kaibel Inscriptiones Graecae Siciliae et Italiae (Berlin, 1890) XIV, no. 1302, pp. 351-2. The most comprehensive modern attempt to disentangle the names of the animals is that of Phillips 1962, where a full discussion of all previous attempts may be found.

4. Suares misread ΜΟΝΟΚΕΝΤΑΥΡΑ for ΗΟΝΟΚΕΝΤΑΥΡΑ , which as Kaibel, op.cit., observed is in fact ἡ ὀνοκένταυρα , the only name written with the definite article. The onocentaur is described by Aelian Περὶ ζῴων ἰδιότητος XVII, 9.

5. A mistake on the part of the copyist is assumed by Petrini (Memorie Prenestine disposte in forma di annali, Rome, 1795, pp. 247-8) and by Pieralisi op.cit, p. 16.

6. Aurigemma 1959, p. 96; for the restorations, see Figs. 37 and 50; Gullini 1956, Tavv. XXIII and XXVI.

7. The necessity of the snake and the birds fitting together has been recognised by Phillips 1962, p. 72, who quotes Pliny N.H. VIII, 14, 36, on bird-catching snakes.

8. Gullini 1956, Tav. XXI.

9. Phillips 1962, p. 69 has suggested that ΞΙΠΙΓ , for ΞΙΦΙC (because of the animal's ferocious snout) was a scholarly guess on the part of the restorers to replace a missing original inscription. He would identify the beast with the ταῦρος σαρκοφάγος of Agatharchides (ed. Müller, col. 1, cap. 76, p. 160) but I do not think this variety of bull with movable horns suits here. The animal looks if anything like a hippopotamus, and one might expect to see this important member of the North African fauna represented somewhere in the upper half of the mosaic. It is rather surprising, however, to find it standing on top of a rocky outcrop: but most of the important, and labelled, animals in this section are shown thus, as free-standing units which are not really integrated into their landscape surroundings, and this may reflect the upper half's piecemeal derivation from book illustrations where each beast was shown in isolation. The combination of a toothy, pointed snout reminiscent of a crocodile's with a rear not unlike that of the accurately-depicted hippopotamus at bottom left of the mosaic suggests that this is a beast of mixed pedigree, perhaps one of the fabulous animals of the

upper half. Similarly, that other quintessentially Nilotic animal, the crocodile, shown in the lower half, is represented in the upper by the fabulous crocodilopard and the smaller land-crocodile, κροκόδειλος χερσαῖος, perhaps to be identified with the skink (described by Pliny N.H. VIII, 38, 91; cf. N.H. XXVIII, 30, 119).

10. Aurigemma 1959, Fig. 48; Gullini 1956, Tav. XXV. Suares' reading is attributable to the defective writing VABOYC in the copy.

11. The rock formations occasionally suggest animal forms — cf. in this piece at the top right below the kneeling archer the shaded part of the rock looks like the rear of an animal.

12. cf. Gullini 1956, Tav. XXV.

13. cf. the treatment of the rocks and water below the temple with obelisks at the left-hand side of the mosaic.

14. cf. p. 71.

15. Although some patches of water are indicated in this shade by the copyist, the water in the mosaic is almost always depicted with horizontal strigilations which the mosaicist occasionally omits when there is too much other detail (e.g. above the roof of the temple in the foreground with soldiers before it). This is a fairly reliable criterion for distinguishing similarly-coloured sky or water, and though the horizontal lines could be missing here, I think the patch is more likely to be meant for sky than water.

16. The extraordinary animal which appears upside-down beneath the giraffe's inscription seems impossible to identify: Phillips 1962, p. 175 has tentatively suggested a variety of porcupine, but this is unlikely; if anything it looks like an ant-eater. Shaw (p. 427 of op.cit. p. 77, n. 1) took it for the giraffe's calf, lying "as if it were just dropt from it".

17. Suares omits ΛΥΝΞ and ΑΓΕΛΑΡΥ from the right of the picture.

18. Gullini 1956, Tav. XXIV.

19. A reading suggested by Phillips 1962, pp. 81-3, following Franz and Pieralisi. He would apply it, however, to the figure of the hunter shooting at the boars below, as "leader of the hunters"; this seems unlikely, though the space to the right may have been occupied by the figure of a hunter rather than an animal.

20. Perhaps for ΚΗΠΙΟΝ , (= a diminutive of κῆπος / κῆφος , a variety of monkey), as suggested by Phillips 1962, pp. 142-4.

21. Attempts to attach ΕΦΛΛΟC to the inscription of the animal above (? σαῦρος πηχυαῖος) are not very convincing; there seems no reason why the mosaicist should have split a name thus, and it is more likely that it belongs to a now vanished animal to the left. Phillips 1962, pp. 91-5, recalling the "Elephas, Rhinoceros" of the Cesi/Stelluti account (cf. p. 6) has ingeniously proposed the reading ΕΛΕΦΑC However, since the letters run right up to the edge of the copy, there

may well have been more in front, and a . . . . ΚΕΦΑΛΟϹ name may be the solution: a smaller animal such as the κυνοκέφαλος would occupy the available space more suitably than would an elephant.

22. Suares has omitted ΑΡΚΟϹ and misread ϹΑΤΤΥΟϹ (perhaps for ϹΑΤΥΡΟϹ, as suggested by Phillips 1962, pp. 162-3, quoting Pliny <u>N.H</u>. VIII, 80, 216; and X, 93, 199).

23. cf. Aurigemma 1959, fig. 52; Gullini 1956, Tav. XXVI.

24. cf. p. 72.

25. The copy unfortunately preserves no more of the name of this problem animal than does the mosaic at present; it is generally identified as the ΧΟΙΡΟΠΙΘΗΚΟϹ of Aristotle <u>H.A</u>. 2, 11 (503a19). There is no reason to suppose that the mosaic did not undergo some repairs in antiquity, so the writing may have been defective when the copyist saw it, or the mosaicists may even have bungled it to start with. The various lapses of orthography and letter-formation in the upper part of the mosaic seems to give the lie to those who have seen it as the work of imported Greek (and in particular Alexandrian) craftsmen: for instance, in no. 6, ΚΗΠΙΕΝ perhaps for ΚΗΠΙΟΝ (see above, n. 20) and ϹΑΥ ΟϹ ΤϹΙΙΧΙϹΝΙΕ perhaps for ϹΑΥΡΟϹ ΠΙΙΧΥΑΙΟϹ; in no. 7 ϹΑΤΤΥΟϹ for perhaps ϹΑΤΥΡΟϹ (see n. 22); in no. 9 the second rho of ΡΙΝΟΚΕΡΩϹ appears as Ｋ; the form of alpha employed is variable: Α and Α in ΗΟΝΟΚΕΝΤΑΥΡΑ and Α in ΘΩΑΝΤΕϹ (no. 1), Δ and Α in ΑΓΕΛΑΡΥ (no. 6) and Δ in ΑΡΚΟϹ (no. 7). Unless these errors and inconsistencies arose from the difficulty of manoeuvring the tiny chips of stone to form the letters, or are the result of ancient restoration work, they look like the handiwork of a non-Greek-reading mosaicist following an illustration or a copy-book.

26. From Aurigemma 1957, Fig. 25 and Gullini 1956, Tav. XVIII it can be seen that the vegetation is original, the tower restored.

27. Some of these details correspond with the plate in Suares' <u>Praenestes Antiquae Libri Duo</u> (see above, p. 84 , n. 46) which shows this part of the mosaic, but it seems unlikely that the latter is connected with 11483, since it shows a larger extent of the scene and is stylistically quite different.

28. As may also be the case with the join in no. 11.

29. Aurigemma 1959, Fig. 21; Gullini 1956, Tav. XIX.

30. The top has been joined in an unlikely way to a patch of vegetation above: cf. p. 17.

31. In the absence of this drawing Suares' description was tentatively applied to no. 15, the copy which is missing from his list: Phillips 1962, p. 105.

32. The plant here appears much as it does in the mosaic now, vertical and level with the woman's body; in no. 13, however, it is shown rather differently, larger and set slightly diagonally, level with her legs. The restorers have in fact inserted a stumpy bush at this point and joined it to the original palm.

33. The only comparable figure elsewhere in the mosaic is the extreme right-hand man in no. 8 holding a trident in his left hand, and it may be this figure which the artist has begun to sketch, attempting to link no. 14 with no. 8, which terminates at the right-hand side with the vertical wall of a tower descending to a two-step stylobate — the requirements which the left-hand side of no. 14 apparently needs. Having started to draw this in he may then have rejected the idea (the stylobate in no. 8 comes to a well-defined end) and considered the alternative of no. 13.

34. If this is a temple it is an odd construction, consisting as it does of nothing but a portico; one expects to see a prostyle temple like the two examples further up and to the left. Drawing no. 13 shows the termination of the roof above the pilaster, so there can be no question of further building behind having been lost in restoration. It would seem to be a shrine rather than a complete temple: cf. F. Studniczka Das Symposion Ptolemaios II (Sächsischen Gesellschaft der Wissenschaft, Phil-hist.kl. Abh. 30, II, Leipzig, 1914) pp. 79-80; and below, p. 73 and n. 15.

35. Aurigemma 1959, Fig. 30; Gullini 1956, Tav. XIX.

36. Aurigemma ibid.; Gullini ibid.

37. Naples, Museo Nazionale inv. 1107; G. Botti Bollettino d'Arte 48, 1963, p. 3. The similarity between the two objects was brought to my notice by Professor J. R. Harris.

38. In the top is an opening 16 cm square, closed with a bronze plate.

39. V. de Tran tam Tinh Le culte des divinités orientales à Herculanum (E.P.R.O. 17, Leiden, 1971) Cat. no. 2, pp. 52-5, pls. III-IV. Botti thought that it was a statue base, but Tran tam Tinh has pointed out that it is too light to take a statue. An interesting alternative to the candelabrum which now appears was proposed by L. Castiglione, "Griechisch-ägyptische Studien: Beiträge zue Deutung des Mosaiks von Präneste", Acta Antiqua A.S.H. 5, 1957, pp. 209-20, who thought that the original should be a cult-image of Osiris Canopus, and the candelabrum was a mistake on the part of the mosaicist. Castiglione identified the base on which the candelabrum stands with the rectangular wooden stretcher with a pole at each corner, from the Temple of Pnepheros at Theadelphia (now in the Musée Gréco-Romaine, Alexandria: E. Breccia Monuments de l'Égypte Gréco-Romaine I, Bergamo, 1926, p. 109 and pls. LV, LVI), but this does not take account of the box-like part. Most recently the architecture of this scene has been described as a "propylaea sheltering a boat-procession" (A. M. Badawy "The Approach to the Egyptian Temple in the Late and Graeco-Roman periods", Z.A.S. 102, 1975, pp. 79-90, in particular p. 86 and Fig. 7). Although the procession of priests and the object which they are carrying are indeed reminiscent of Ptolemaic scenes of sacred boats carried on stretchers, there is unfortunately no boat present in this case, at least in the copy or the restored mosaic; however, the little kiosk is probably the sort of way-station which Badawy discusses: see especially pp. 86-7 for the situation of such kiosks "above the lake" ("tp š") and their connection with ceremonies of landing or sailing off, and cf. below, p. 73 and n. 15.

It is interesting to note Poussin's observations in connection with this object, for he incorporated several motifs from the mosaic in "The Holy Family in Egypt", painted 1655-7, in order to fix the locality; the kiosk and priests appear in the background, turned sideways-on to the spectator. The artist had his own ideas as to what the chest-like object might be: "le coffre nommé Soro Apin ou estoint enfermés les reliques et ossemens de Serapin leur dieu ...." (in a letter to Chantelou, quoted by A. Blunt, op.cit. in n. 47, p. 85,, pp. 310-12; see also Ragna Enking Der Apis-Altar Johann Melchior Dinglingers, Glückstadt-Hamburg-New York, 1939, pp. 28-30). The background to this idea has been traced by Charles G. Dempsey in his article on Poussin's use of Egyptian motifs ("Poussin and Egypt", The Art Bulletin 45, 1963, pp. 109-19, especially 109-13) — a contemporary derivation of Serapis from σορός, sarcophagus, and Apis. Unfortunately, Dempsey is probably right in concluding that Poussin worked from Dal Pozzo's copies and not the original mosaic, otherwise he would be a corroborative witness to the fact that there was no object on top of the naos-like base.

40. cf. Aurigemma 1959, Fig. 27; Gullini 1956, Tav. XIX. The restored area exceeds that shown in either illustration.

41. cf. Aurigemma 1959, Fig. 5; Gullini 1956, Tav. XIII.

42. "Il Cardinal Magalotto . . . riserbato per se un solo pezzo, qual donò al Gran Duca...." — see above, p. 7.

43. Aurigemma 1959, pp. 59-62; see also M. Cagiano de Azevedo "Il piu antico restauro al musaico Barberini", Bollettino dell'Istituto Centrale del Restauro 13, 1953, p. 62, cf. Lumbroso op.cit., pp. 171-2.

44. "When I saw it I was astounded, and I bought it forthwith." A. F. Gori Inscriptionum Antiquarum Graecarum et Romanarum quae in Etruriae Urbibus exstant, Pars Tertia, Florence, 1743, Tab. III and pp. XLVIII-LIV; the quotation is on p. LIII. Gori included an illustration of the fragment in his work, and had meanwhile asked friends in Rome to check the original to see if this part were missing. However, before their answer came he was forced, "typographo urgente", to send his manuscript to press, concluding therein that his piece was perhaps one of those left in the apse of the Bishop's Palace (taking Suares' account as an indication of parts surviving there at the time of his writing).

45. R. Engelmann "Das Mosaik von Palestrina", Archäologische Zeitung 32, 1875, pp. 127-34 and Taf. 12; Engelmann seemed to know of the existence of the Palestrina drawings in England for he says: "Und trotz alledem erwartete ich, um ein endgültiges Urtheil aussprechen zu können, noch die Gelegenheit die Zeichnung des Cav. dal Pozzo, die Lanciani in London gesehen haben will, zu vergleichen." (p. 130). But there seems to have been some confusion here, and Lanciani may have been looking for the drawings among those of Dal Pozzo's which came to the British Museum via the Franks Collection, see earlier, p. 87, n. 62.

46. See earlier, p. 7 ; if the "Notizie di diverse anticaglie" are all Dal Pozzo's it would be strange for him not to refer the drawing as his own.

47. Aurigemma 1959, Fig. 13: a well-defined line runs around the inner copy and the outer filling-in.

48. Minor points of divergence being the number of crossings of the pergola's lattice work at the top, or the form of the fence at the right-hand side which the artist has simplified.

Chapter III

1. Hence perhaps the designation "disegni di casa", cf. p. 7 ; contra this, however, is the account quoted further down on p. 7.

2. See Gullini 1956, Tav. II; the possible lacunae in the Nilotic mosaic are discussed by Aurigemma 1959, pp. 92ff.

3. See p. 9.

4. The shape of the upper half has been slightly altered since that time: the seventeenth-century restorers gave it an elliptical arch which indented before joining the main straight-sided part of the mosaic, but these indentations have now been filled in.

5. Gullini 1956, pp. 7-8 takes the view that it did not extend into the niches because the floor level of the latter slopes to allow the water to run down; but he acknowledges that its present shape is due entirely to the Barberini restoration. For the outline of the Fish Mosaic, see Gullini 1956, Tav. II and Delbrueck, op.cit. (p. 77, n. 3), Taf. X; it was contained by a strip of concrete designed to hold in the water flowing over its surface. It has sometimes been suggested that the niches were occupied by statues of Fortuna, Jupiter and Juno (see, e.g., H. von Heintze Gymnasium 63, 1956, p. 536), but this idea is of necessity tied to the identification of the apse as the site of the Praenestine oracle, cf. n. 7 on p. 78.

6. See the plan, Delbrueck ibid., Taf. XV; the niches are irregular, that in the centre being 1.50 m wide x 0.80 m deep, those at either side 1.35-1.36 m with a maximum depth of 1.4 m. In his Memorie Prenestine ... (see n. 5 on p. 89) Petrini gives in Tav. II a plan of the apse and the restored mosaic which shows the latter almost filling the available space; the dimensions which he employs, however, are 30 x 22.5 Roman palms for the apse (6.7 x 5.02 m) and 26 x 21 for the restored mosaic (5.81 x 4.7 m).

7. The dog is looking at something to the right where there is no longer any figure or object, a discrepancy noted by Schmidt 1929, p. 31.

8. Cf. above, p. 7 .

9. Phillips 1962, pp. 198-224; cf. Schmidt 1929, pp. 22-25. Phillips suggests that the source of the upper half of the mosaic is an illustrated treatise on Ethiopian animals of a date not later than the second century

B.C. and possibly connected with Ptolemy II; the same tradition of animal depiction is reflected in the painted friezes of the Marissa tomb (J. P. Peters and H. Thiersch Painted Tombs in the Necropolis of Marissa, London, 1905) and in an illustrated manuscript of Oppian Cynegetica of the tenth or eleventh century A.D. but traceable to earlier sources. The mosaic's possible derivation from an illustrated zoological work of Hellenistic date had already been suggested by M. I. Rostovtzeff The Social and Economic History of the Hellenistic World (Oxford, 1953), p. 318; and the problem of its derivation from book-illustration or painted frieze has been touched upon by Karl Schefold in "Probleme der Pompejanischen Malerei", R.M. 72, 1965, pp. 116-26, especially 120ff.

10. cf. Phillips 1962, pp. 115ff. for this concept of "Egypt...connected to Ethiopia by means of the Nile".

11. For the possible content of no. 14, compare perhaps the fragment of wall-painting, regrettably hard to decipher, from the Isiac sanctuary below S. Sabina on the Aventine: it shows a boat bearing some unidentifiable object pulling into a jetty on which stand some figures (F. Darsy Recherches archéologiques à Sainte-Sabine sur l'Aventin, Vatican City, 1968, pl. D and pp. 49ff.

12. See above, p. 72.

13. It is not easy to hazard a guess at what these bystanders might be watching because there is no comparable pictorial material; the Palestrina mosaic is to date unique in much of its subject matter. A parallel that might be offered is the tantalisingly fragmentary mosaic excavated in the Via Nazionale, Rome, in 1882 and now in the Antiquario Comunale (M. E. Blake M.A.A.R. 17, 1940, pl. 20, fig. 3 and p. 104). The pavement of which this piece formed the bottom left-hand corner must have been a compilation of scenes not entirely dissimilar to those in the Palestrina example and like the latter, to which it is technically much inferior, it seems to derive from some earlier or better tradition when set beside the bulk of Roman Egyptianising material. The surviving piece shows spectators at the ceremony of feeding the sacred crocodiles on some festive occasion, a popular tourist attraction which is both represented elsewhere (a sculptured base in the Vatican: see M. Malaise Inventaire préliminaire des documents égyptiens découverts en Italie, E.P.R.O. 21, Leiden, 1972, no. 310, pp. 168-9) and attested in literature (at Arsinoe: Strabo XVII, 1, 38; cf. A. S. Hunt and C. C. Edgar Select Papyri II, Loeb ed., London, 1934, no. 416).

14. In no. 17 the gaze of the people at the right-hand side could be directed merely at the passing warship but seems to extend beyond this — they might be focussing on the event in no. 14.

15. cf. A. Badawy's observations on the placing of kiosks or way-stations in the vicinity of a landing quay, Z.A.S. 102, 1975, pp. 86-7; the building with soldiers before it and the associated architecture was compared by M. I. Rostovtzeff, R.M. 26, 1911, p. 61 n. 1, with the remains of a festival pavilion on Lake Mareotis.

16. The join between the rock, the walled complex and the tower above has also been suggested by Kyle M. Phillips in his proposed reconstruction of the mosaic: Phillips 1962, p. 110.

17. See above, p. 72.

18. Suares *op.cit.*, p. 289.

ABBREVIATIONS

Aurigemma 1959	S. Aurigemma "Il restauro di consolidamento del Mosaico Barberini, condotto nel 1952", Rend. P.A.R.A. Ser. III, 30-31, 1957-9, pp. 41-98.
Gullini 1956	G. Gullini I mosaici di Palestrina (Archeologia Classica, vol. supp. I), Rome, 1956.
Schmidt 1929	E. Schmidt Studien zum Barberinischen Mosaik in Palestrina (Zur Kunstgeschichte des Auslandes, 127), Strassburg, 1929.
Acta Ant. A.S.H.	Acta Antiqua Academiae Scientiarum Hungaricae, Budapest.
A.J.A.	American Journal of Archaeology.
Bull. Com.	Bullettino della Commissione Archeologica Comunale di Roma.
Diss. P.A.R.A.	Atti della Pontificia Accademia Romano di Archeologia, Dissertazioni.
E.P.R.O.	Études préliminaries aux religions orientales dans l'empire Romain.
J.d.I.	Jahrbuch des Deutschen Archäologischen Instituts.
M.A.A.R.	Memoirs of the American Academy in Rome.
Mem. Linc.	Atti della Accademia Nazionale dei Lincei, Memorie.
P.B.S.R.	Papers of the British School at Rome.
R.A.	Revue Archéologique.
RE	Paulys Realencyclopädie der classischen Altertumswissenschaft. Neue Bearbeitung.
Rend. Linc.	Atti della Accademia Nazionale dei Lincei, Rendiconti.
Rend. P.A.R.A.	Atti della Pontificia Accademia Romana di Archeologia, Rendiconti.
R.M.	Mitteilungen des Deutschen Archäologischen Instituts. Römische Abteilung.
Z.A.S.	Zeitschrift für Agyptische Sprache und Altertumskunde.

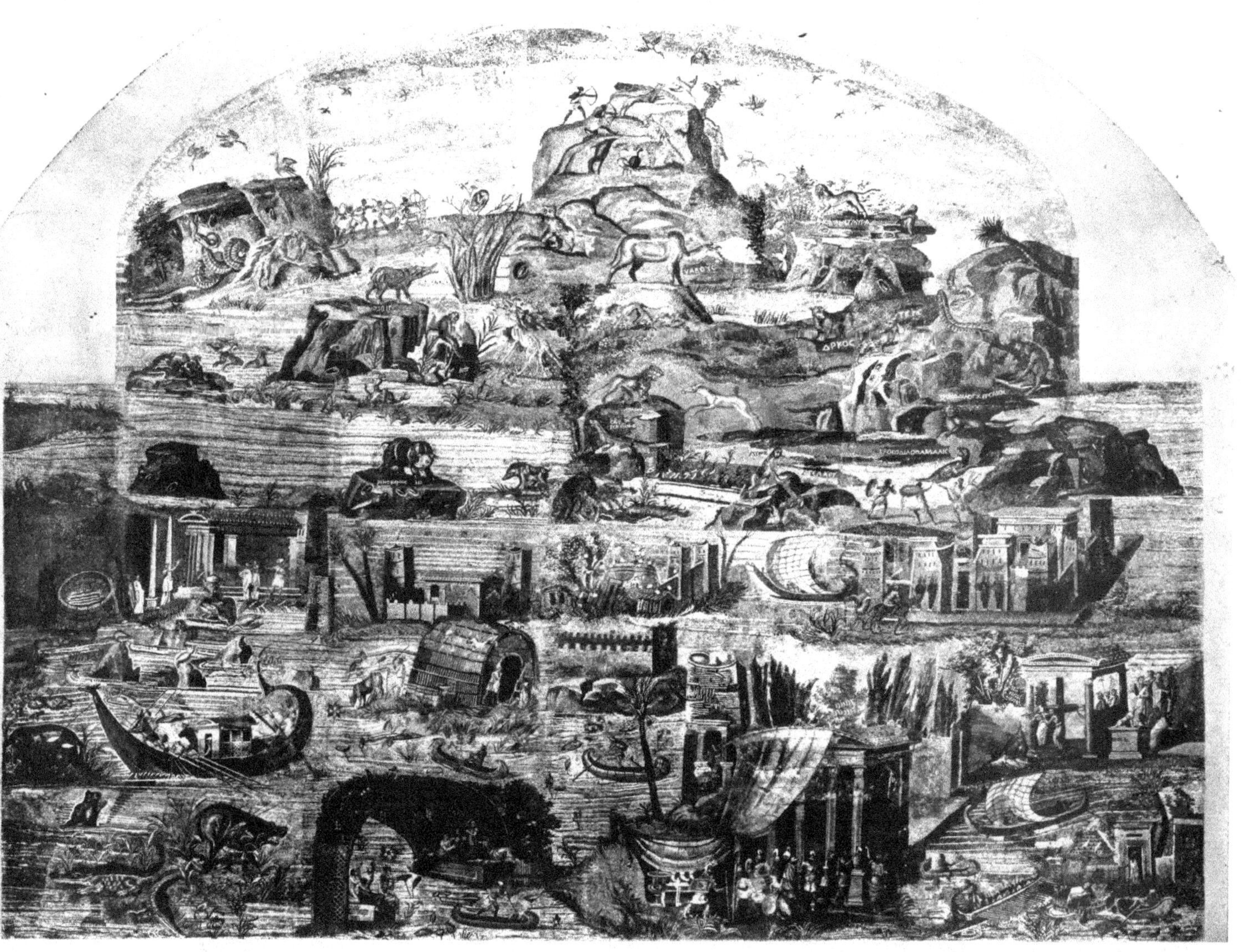

Please note that a full-size version of this page is available to download from www.barpublishing.com/additional-downloads.html
The original foldout has been reduced in size to match the A4 format of this book, the image is therefore not as clear as the original foldout. Please refer to the original foldout via the download for the original content.

Please also be aware that the image might be cut off or not complete in the printed book.

www.ingramcontent.com/pod-product-compliance
Lightning Source LLC
LaVergne TN
LVHW070409110826
845147LV00017B/978